How to Win

IN THE

CHESS OPENINGS

BY

I. A. Horowitz

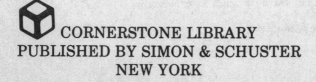

CORNERSTONE LIBRARY
PUBLISHED BY SIMON & SCHUSTER
NEW YORK

Published by Cornerstone Library
A Division of Simon & Schuster, Inc.
Simon & Schuster Building
1230 Avenue of the Americas
New York, New York 10020

CORNERSTONE LIBRARY and colophon are registered
trademarks of Simon & Schuster, Inc.

This new Cornerstone Library edition is published by arrangement with David
McKay Company, Inc. and is a complete and unabridged reprint of the
original hardcover edition.

Manufactured in the United States of America

ISBN 0-346-12445-X

Contents

Foreword

Ever since the first game of chess was recorded—about five hundred years ago or more—no less than twenty thousand chess books, written in different languages, have appeared in print. Consequently, every phase of the game has been considered.

Yet here is another book. . . . Why?

In delving through multitudinous works on chess openings, I have come to the conclusion that only one thing is clear. And that is that all is quiet confusion! The reader is required to memorize an opening by rote, is occasionally told via the symbol of an exclamation point or question mark that a move is good, bad or indifferent, and then is left hanging, as it were, in mid air to reason out for himself the whys and wherefores. What part each move plays in the strategic concept of the opening pattern is lightly glossed over or not mentioned at all.

Under the circumstances, there has been room for improvement. In this book, I have, therefore, endeavored to present the study of chess openings in a logical, easy-to-understand manner, not beyond the grasp of the player who has learned little more than the rules of chess. To begin with, I have outlined and discussed the principles and concepts of opening play, common to all openings, Then, in turn, I have taken specifically, each of the most popular openings— attacks and defenses—and have broken them down to their individual moves and grand plans. I have tried to show how the tactical forte of each move ties up with the strategical idea. Lastly, I have appended to each opening a classic, over-the-board, example from actual play in "movie" style.

For those unfamiliar with the term "chess movie," I wish to point out that it is no more than a chess game, recorded by a series of diagrams. The numerous diagrams make for clarity as well as ease of study. For the "movie" obviates the use of a chessboard and men, as the game can be followed from the text.

In closing, I wish to give a word of caution: gaining an advantage in the opening brings victory in the endgame. I must confess, however, that the title has given me a pang of conscience. What I really ought to call the book is "How to Understand the Chess Openings." Most players, however, are not interested in understanding; they only want to win. Hence the title. It is clear that with understanding will come many victories.

I. A. Horowitz

1

The original position from which the opening springs is the most difficult of the entire game. For here thirty-two potent units are animated and unleash a vast power.

Principles of Opening Play

THE game of chess is divided into three parts—the opening, the middle game and the endgame. The divisions are purely arbitrary, merely for the purpose of facilitating study. No dividing line separates the parts; the transition from the opening to the middle game and from the middle game to the endgame is indicated by the action and the number of men remaining on the board.

The opening covers approximately the first twelve moves of the game, with all or most of the pieces on the board. The middle game is characterized generally by the presence of

Queens; the endgame is greatly simplified, with few of the forces remaining.

The opening is a development of forces. It begins with the first move and ends with the mobilization of nearly all of the men. The Rooks, as a rule, are the last to enter the skirmish, and often do not participate in the play until well into the middle game.

TYPICAL OPENING POSITIONS

Queen's Gambit Declined with Rooks developed.

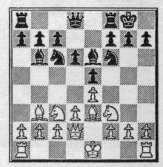

Giuoco Piano—White's Rooks not yet moved.

Ultimate Goal vs. Opening Goal

In order to understand the mechanics of the opening, it is necessary to know the opening goal. While checkmate is the principal goal of the game, it is subordinated in the opening, since the pieces are just beginning to get out. Of course, if the opponent plays very badly, or exposes his King critically or neglects his development glaringly, then checkmating ideas come to the forefront. With reasonably correct play by both contestants, lesser objectives are the goal. These all tie in with the prime purpose—checkmate of the opponent's King. Checkmate is the ultimate goal.

Try for Small Advantages

Opening play can contribute towards the checkmating goal in a minor way. Essentially, it can do so by laying a sound foundation for the middle and endgame; by gaining small po-

EXAMPLES OF RATIONAL AND IRRATIONAL DEVELOPMENT

Ruy Lopez—Rational development on both sides. Checkmate is a consideration far in the future.

Ruy Lopez—. . . N-B6 mate. Violations of opening principles have brought a sudden end.

sitional and material advantages. Many small advantages add up to a large plus.

What is a sound foundation and what are the small advantages? The answers to these questions shed light on the function of opening moves.

A sound foundation is one which is free of structural weaknesses, weaknesses which require attention or which undermine anything built upon them. As the foundation pertains only to Pawns, the subject is better treated in a discussion of the endgame. Insofar as the foundation affects the opening, however, a limited discussion will appear later on.

More to the point is the question of small advantages. What are they?

There are two types of advantage in chess. One is positional; the other material.

Positional advantage is the plus which derives from the ability to control squares, vital for immediate or future action, as well as from the sounder Pawn structure. Superior mobility and command of greater terrain augment the advantage.

Control of the Center

While the opening is concerned with every conceivable advantage, emphasis is generally placed on the control of impor-

EXAMPLES OF POSITIONAL ADVANTAGE

Black's men are hemmed in behind his own lines. White enjoys operating space.

Black is a piece to the good. He lacks the time, however, to stave off mate.

Black suffers from chronic structural weaknesses. His Queen-side Pawns are not self-supporting.

Black's backward King Pawn is a vulnerable target. Soon White will attack it again and again.

tant squares. In the absence of outright blunders ceding material, the initial goal is the gain of squares.

There are 64 squares on the chessboard. Half are white and half are black. Except for color distinction, to all appearances they are very much alike. Yet some squares are more valuable than others. Which are the more important squares and why?

As indicated on the diagram, the squares in the center of the board are the more important ones. The reason they are more important becomes apparent when the squares are considered in terms of a network of interlinked paths. It is clear that the player who controls the hub of the network can send his men from one side of the board, directly through the hub, to the other side of the board with ease. Whereas the player who does not control the hub must send his men from one side of the board to the other via devious routes, time-consuming

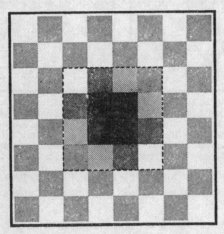

The most important squares are the very centermost (in black). Other squares taper off in importance as indicated on diagram above.

routes. As time is an important factor in chess—that is, as it is important to reach a goal in the least number of moves—it follows that it is important to control the central squares.

Control of the central squares is the primary positional advantage sought for in the opening. It enhances the player's mobility and operating space to the detriment of the opponent. Exploitation of structural weaknesses pertaining to Pawns is a subsidiary objective of the opening. These will be covered later on.

Gain of Material

The gain of squares is a gain of ground over which the chessmen may move. Even more important, however, is the

EXAMPLES OF CENTER CONTROL

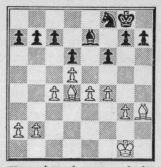

In this position, White is able to utilize his control of the center to institute an overwhelming attack. White plays R-K4, followed by R-N4—typical mid-game advantage.

Here the advantage of the center has been carried to the endgame. White can advance on either or both wings or in the center, while Black must bide his time.

gain of material. For material is force, and a preponderance of force, by its very nature, brooks little or no interference or resistance.

The power of the force of a lowly Pawn may be gleaned from the fact that, in a game between two chessmasters, the advantage of a Pawn is sufficient to win. Hence it is imperative at all times, in the absence of other consideration, to maintain an even or favorable balance of force. The sacrifice of material,

EXAMPLES OF PAWN MINUS

White has sacrificed a Pawn for position. Should his attack fail, White will lose.

This could be the windup of the previous position! The extra Pawn queens.

consequently, should be viewed with suspicion. "Always sacrifice your opponent's pieces" is a sound guiding principle.

In this connection, the table of the relative value of the chessmen is useful. Evaluating a Pawn as a unit of one, the Knight is the equivalent of three units, the Bishop three and a small fraction units, the Rook five and the Queen nine.

As it is not always possible or beneficial to exchange Pawn for Pawn or Knight for Knight, etc., it is well to calculate in an exchange the value of the units given for the units received. Two Rooks, for example, having a total value of ten units, may be considered better than a Queen, whose unit total is nine. A Rook, Bishop and Knight add up to eleven units plus and are clearly more valuable than a Queen.

In the absence of serious blunders, it is almost impossible to gain much material in the opening. Often, however, small profit may be gained by judicious exchanges, such as a Knight for the opponent's Bishop or a Rook for the opponent's Bishop and Knight. These small differences add up and their cumulative effect is a decisive factor in the outcome of the game.

The gain of material, no matter how little, is also the goal of the opening.

Changing Values

In any demonstration, the forces which join the fray may be momentarily more valuable than dormant forces of equal stature. This is particularly true when the King is the target. Thus an active Pawn or Knight, delivering checkmate to the opposing King, or compelling the surrender of material, cannot be given the wooden classification of one or three units. The worth of material at all times is related to the position. All things being equal, the preceding table of values applies.

EXAMPLES OF CHANGING VALUES

Black is a raft of material ahead. He cannot, however, prevent mate, after *1 . . . Q-B2; 2 RxB.*

Black is lost as he cannot save his Bishop Pawn or stop the advance of the White Bishop Pawn.

How to Try for Small Advantages

It is one thing to know the goal; it is another to reach it. The wide gap is bridged by the correct management of the forces.

Correct management requires the application of sound principles. As these, however, are founded on experience and logic, they are not difficult to master.

Technically, the principles fall into two classes—strategy and tactics. Strategy is the plan for obtaining advantages; tactics is the science of executing the plan by disposing of the forces.

As the major goal of the opening is to gain control of the central squares, that is the first strategic plan. As force is the only means of attempting to reach the goal, the principle evolves: *Bring out the forces so that a maximum of power is brought to bear on the central squares in the shortest time.*

Plan Your Development

To execute the plan properly, it is necessary to know in what order the forces should be brought out. Which should come first and which should follow? These are tactical considerations.

EXAMPLES OF PLANNED AND UNPLANNED DEVELOPMENT

White controls the center; King Pawn and Queen Pawn, Knights and Bishops bear down on the vital squares.

Haphazard development with Knights on the wing. Position is far from ideal for either White or Black.

The advance of the King Pawn or Queen Pawn to the fourth rank generally initiates the opening. This is so because the advanced Pawn attacks the central squares and, at the same time, frees the Queen and a Bishop for future action.

Knights First

After the Pawn moves, the minor pieces—Bishops and Knights—follow. Knights should generally be developed before Bishops, and there are sound reasons for this.

At the beginning of the game, the Knight has a range of two squares—R3 and B3. As the King Pawn or Queen Pawn is advanced, the range increases by one square, including either K2 or Q2. Thus, in the first few moves, the Knight enjoys a choice of practically three squares. As the square R3 is almost out of the question—a Knight on R3 does not bear down on the center and controls only half as many squares as at B3—the choice is really of but two squares. Consequently, with only two moves from which to choose, it is easy to determine which of the squares the Knight ought to occupy. The Bishop, on the other hand, has a long range. After the King Pawn has moved, the Bishop could conceivably go to K2, Q3, B4, N5 or R6. R6, of course, is not a good choice, but it is within the realm of possibility. This adds up to four good squares. When it is possible to go to four squares, it is difficult to determine the correct one. When it is possible to go to two squares, it is comparatively easy to determine the correct one. Thus there is practically no guesswork in developing the Knight, while the Bishop moves are subject to doubt. That is one reason why the Knight usually precedes the Bishop.

Another important reason for this sequence is that the Knights on B3 are aggressively posted. They control the central squares, attack hostile Pawns in the center or prevent their advance to the fourth rank.

Then Bishops

All in all, it is clear that the development of the Bishop is best deferred until some such time as its most effective post is determined. When, however, the best square for the Bishop is already known, the Bishop may precede the Knight. In the absence of specific convictions, the Knight comes first.

Major Pieces Later

With the development of the minor pieces—Bishops and Knights—the first strategic plan is nearly complete. As it is necessary, however, to bring as much pressure as possible to bear on the central squares, the major pieces—Rooks and

EXAMPLES OF BISHOP AND KNIGHT DEVELOPMENT

What is the best square for White's King Bishop?

The Knight at KB3 attacks the center and a Pawn.

At K2, the Knight is less aggressive. Moreover, it blocks the King Bishop. Black can seize the initiative with . . . N-KB3, as he attacks a Pawn, controls the center.

A Knight at R3 commands half as many squares as a Knight at B3. Moreover, it does not attack the center. Again . . . N-KB3 gives Black the initiative.

This is the Bishop's Opening. The attack on White's King Pawn gives Black a momentary initiative.

This is the Ruy Lopez. The early Bishop move attacks Black's support of the King Pawn in the center.

Queen—should also assist in the action. That is why, among other reasons, they should be developed.

As Rooks assert themselves best on open files, they should be placed on such files or on files which may reasonably be expected to open during the early course of the game. The King file or the Queen file or both are often most suitable. For these files have been half opened due to the advance of the King Pawn or Queen Pawn. On these files, moreover, the Rooks join the center action. Occasionally, the Bishop files serve as

EXAMPLES OF ROOK DEVELOPMENT

Here White's King Rook pins Black's Knight on the open King file in the early play. Black is already in trouble.

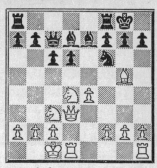

White's best move is to play his King Rook to K1, on a file which may reasonably be expected to open.

White's advanced King Bishop Pawn helps to open the King Bishop file for use by the King Rook.

By placing his Rook on the Queen Bishop file, White exerts pressure on Black's Queen Bishop Pawn.

excellent posts for the Rooks. For, in some openings, the Bishop Pawns advance and give free range to the Rooks.

The Rooks as a rule, get into play slowly and the Queen Rook is about the last to join the action. This sequence is justified by the necessity of contesting control of the center. Pawns and the minor pieces play a major role in this plan.

Function of Castling

In order to be able to bring the Rooks to the King file and also to enable the Rooks to cooperate, the King must get out of the way. As long as the King remains on King square, he not only pre-empts the square K1, but also prevents the Rooks from cooperating. Castling on either wing is the answer. Incidentally, also, castling *should* safeguard the King.

Develop the Queen with Care

The Queen generally assumes a positive role late in the opening. An early Queen sortie is apt to recoil: the Queen will serve as a target, be attacked and be compelled to retreat. The time expended in advancing and retreating will be used by the adversary to bolster his development. Moreover, since the Queen enjoys a wide variety of possibilities, it is difficult to determine its most suitable role. For the same reason that the development of the Bishop is deferred until its best post is known, the Queen should not join the fray until the position has crystallized. Then it is less of a "hit or miss" development.

Plan Soundly from the Start

From the first strategic plan, various propositions develop. It is obvious, for instance, that if a maximum power is to be brought to bear on the central squares in the shortest time, a haphazard development which fails to exert pressure on the center is a violation of principle. It is also clear that a unit

EXAMPLES OF LOSS OF TIME IN THE OPENING

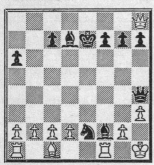
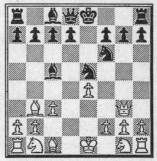

White's Queen has wandered over the board, picking up stray material. Black, however, mates in three, beginning with *1 . . . QxPch.*

White's Queen has moved three times, while Black has brought out his pieces. Black now wins White's Queen with *1 . . . BxPch!*

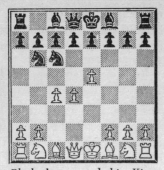 

Black has moved his King Knight three times. Now Black must lose a piece, thus: 1 P-Q5, NxKP; 2 P-B5 and the Knight is trapped.

Black has lost time by Pawn-grabbing with 1 . . . BxQBP. He loses a piece after 2 Q-K2! for White threatens both 3 N-Q6 mate and 3 QxB.

should not be moved more than once in the opening, unless there is good reason for doing so. Two or more moves by the same unit, as a rule, are the equivalent of wasting opportunities to bring out more force. In fact, only special reasons will ever justify any deviation from the main plan—control of the center with a preponderance of quickly developed force.

When possible, the ideal placement for all units should be visualized before any one is moved. When that is not possible, then the choice and location of the unit to be moved should be judged on principle—in relation to the first strategic plan.

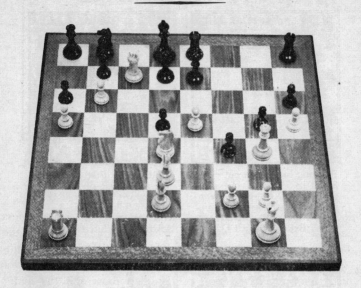

2

Exceptions to the First Principle

As was explained in the previous chapter, the first strategic principle points up the necessity for bringing maximum power to bear on the central squares in the shortest time. Likewise, it points out the fallacy of deviating from principle. Yet, while to toe the line with rigid obedience may be good discipline, it is wooden, unimaginative chess.

To Do or Not to Do?

Occasionally, during the opening stages of a game, an opportunity presents itself to pick off an opponent's Pawn or to go after his King. These pursuits are in violation of principle. For it is hardly possible to go Pawn-grabbing or checkmating and, at the same time, give the required attention to proper

EXAMPLES OF UNJUSTIFIED RISKS

Bringing his Queen out early, Black has violated one principle. Now he goes Pawn-grabbing and loses his Queen: *1 ... QxP; 2 Q-N5ch, P-B3; 3 BxPch, KxB; 4 QxQ.*

White hopes that Black will miss the threat of mate. But Black now plays *1 ... Q-K2* and soon follows with *... N-KB3* and gains time by attacking the White Queen.

EXAMPLES OF JUSTIFIED RISKS

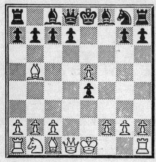

White has mismanaged his forces. That is why Black can afford to grab a Pawn: *1 ... P-B3; 2 B-QB4, Q-R4ch; 3 N-B3, QxKP,* yet expect to escape with a whole skin.

White's Queen has moved early and moves again: *1 QxPch, KxQ; 2 B-R6ch, K-N1; 3 R-N6ch, RPxR; 4 N-B6 mate.* Black's early Queen moves justify White's.

development. Still a Pawn is a Pawn, and the King is the King. These are important considerations. Surely, if the target is the opposing monarch and if it can be ascertained with a reasonable degree of certainty that he will topple from his throne, then definitely it is correct to violate principle. Checkmate leaves no weaknesses in its wake. If, however, the target is a Pawn and even if its successful capture is assured, the consequences of the action should be further appraised in the light of its effect on the entire position. In the quest for immediate material gain, the strategic plan is bound to suffer. To appraise the gain of material against loss of position requires inordinate skill.

In the opening, Pawn-grabbing expeditions or premature mating attacks are apt to boomerang. Temptation in these directions should be resisted. One thing is certain, if the opponent has not violated any principles, any rash action is foredoomed. If he has violated principles, a calculated risk is justifiable.

OTHER PRINCIPLES

Besides the first strategic principle, there are other principles of chess common to all openings. Their application paves the way to opening goals.

Principle of Mobility

A piece which cannot move is a useless piece.

The potential force of a Queen is nine times as great as that of a Pawn. Its actual force depends on other considerations. Its ability to participate in the fray is the main one. If a Queen is bottled up and an opposing Pawn threatens mate which cannot be stopped, the Pawn—in this instance—is of greater actual value than the Queen. Similarly, the value of all the chessmen is modified by their ability to participate in the fray.

Force, of itself, is potential. Enclosed in a Queen or Bishop or Rook or Knight or Pawn, it is enclosed in just another piece of wood. To unleash its powers, avenues of action are essential. These avenues are technically called mobility.

To gain maximum utility of the chessmen, diagonals should be open for Bishops; files and ranks for the Rooks; files, ranks and diagonals for the Queen; and a choice of posts should exist for the Knights; Pawns should not be hindered in their forward

In this position, Black's Queen is practically worthless. Almost any White assault is apt to succeed.

Because of the awkward position of the Black men, White mates in two moves: QxBch, NxQ; 2 N-K6 mate.

movement. Files, ranks, diagonals and open squares are the avenues of action for the chessmen.

Principle of Diversion

Forces decoyed are forces destroyed.

Often during the course of a game, a situation arises where a player threatens to gain a preponderance of force in a vital sector. To meet force equally with force in the selfsame sector is the most effective countermeasure. But this is not always possible. When it is not possible, some other means must be found to parry the threat.

The establishment of threats in another sector may be the answer. These counter threats may be of sufficient real or psychological importance to divert the enemy forces from their contemplated action, or they may defer the enemy action long enough to gain time in which to work out a permanent solution against it.

As attacks in chess occur in the center or on the wings, the principle of diversion as applied works as follows: an attack on the wing is met by a counter-attack in the center or on the other wing; an attack in the center is met by a counter-attack on the wing.

Diversion is necessary only when the attack cannot be met

EXAMPLES OF DIVERTING FORCES

This position from an actual game is an example of diversion. White's King-side attack is gaining momentum and Black counters on the Queen-side in hope of drawing off White's forces from his King.

White's center is weak and subject to further attack. So he diverts the play to the King-side: *1* RxP*ch*, KxR; *2* R-N1*ch*, K-B3; *3* Q-N5*ch*, K-K3; *4* R-K1*ch*, K-Q2; *5* Q-B5*ch*, K-Q3; *6* Q-B5*ch*, K-Q2; *7* B-B5 mate.

adequately by direct means, such as an attack in the center by a defense in the center, or a wing attack by a wing defense.

Principle of Give and Take

Better location is compensation.

Every move in chess gives up something and takes something in return. The move *1* P-K4, for instance, gives up control of the squares KB3 and Q3 by the King Pawn. In return, however, the move gains control of the squares KB5 and Q5 and

GIVE AND TAKE

The move *1* P-K4 adds a net plus to the position. For control of the central squares Q5 and KB5 is of greater value than loss of the control (by the King Pawn) of the squares Q3 and KB3. Every move in chess carries some minus as well as plus value.

also frees the Bishop and Queen for future action. As control of the central squares is of greater value than loss of control of the other squares, the move *1 P-K4* adds a net plus to the position.

Similarly, every move on the chessboard involves a sacrifice and a gain. It is a mistaken notion to think only in terms of gain. It is essential, however to weigh the gain against the loss in the light of immediate and future prospects.

The Move P-R3?

That practical nonentity of a move, P-R3, is not a principle; it is merely a move. It crops up, however, time and again in most games of chess and is therefore worthy of a note. Generally, it is of doubtful value; for it violates the principle of rapid development. A piece might be brought into action during the time it takes to play P-R3. Moreover, it does not bear down directly on the central squares and often even causes a slight but irreparable weakness in the Pawn structure.

Oddly enough, despite these drawbacks, there is purpose in the puny P-R3. It provides an exit for the King; it prevents an enemy pin or incursion; it is a prop for a Pawn advance; it is a clearance of the square R2 for a retreat or a maneuvering point—and, most wonderful of all, it is sometimes an attacking move.

White may play P-KR3 to prevent the pin ... B-N5 and to restrict the movement of Black's Queen Bishop.

The actions of both White's and Black's King Knights at B3 are paralyzed because of the respective pins.

All of which confounds the issue. Is P-R3 good or bad? Unfortunately, there is no inflexible, ironclad rule, covering all cases. Adroit evasion is the answer. The move P-R3 is good when there is nothing better.

THE FOUNDATION

The Pawn skeleton forms the basic foundation of the chess opening. The original position presents a Pawn line in solid array. Each Pawn enjoys security and mobility.

As the Pawns advance towards the enemy, they are stronger because more threatening but also they are endangered and restricted. They form distinctive patterns around which the pieces rally to give character to the opening.

A — Pawn Weaknesses

IF A weakness develops in the Pawn structure, it may lead to serious difficulties. A weakness requires attention and places an added burden on the balance of the forces. It diverts force from the normal course and consequently lessens pressure in some sector. Weaknesses, therefore, should be avoided.

Which are the weaknesses pertinent to Pawns?

EXAMPLES OF DOUBLED PAWNS

White's doubled Queen Bishop Pawn is unwieldy, hard to protect.

The opened King Rook file compensates for the doubled Pawn.

The Doubled Pawn

The doubled Pawn may be weak. It often suffers from lack of mobility. As a rule, it controls only half as many *vital* squares as two Pawns, lined up side by side. At times, however, the doubled Pawn offers a measure of compensation in the file which its displacement has opened.

The Backward Pawn

The backward Pawn is weak. It is a Pawn which hardly participates in the fray and shirks its normal assignment. Since it is more or less fixed, it becomes an easy, lasting target.

Black's Queen Bishop Pawn is backward.

Black's Queen Pawn is backward.

The Isolated Pawn

The isolated Pawn is weak. It is a Pawn which cannot be guarded by another Pawn. When attacked, it must be guarded by a minor or major piece. Hence it engenders a waste of force.

Over-extended Pawns

The foregoing is pertinent to single Pawns or, in the case of the doubled Pawn, to two Pawns. There are also weaknesses which are inherent in a group of Pawns. They stem mainly from the "one-way traffic" feature of a Pawn.

A Pawn can advance; it cannot retreat. Hence every Pawn move, to a certain extent, engenders two weaknesses. Its ad-

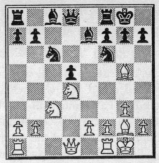

White's isolated Queen Pawn requires constant protection by forces, which otherwise might be used elsewhere.

The target is Black's isolated Queen Pawn. Its defense diverts Black men from more useful action.

vance brings it closer to the enemy, where it can be more readily attacked, and it is removed one step further away from its own men, where the natural protection which they afford is diminished. As the Pawn cannot retreat, any weakness in its wake requires reinforcement by the rest of the forces.

Occasionally, a group of Pawns will advance in an assault. The target is big game, often the opposing King. As long as the assault is successful, it matters little whether the Pawns are strong or weak or whether the Pawns are afforded or afford protection or not. If the assault fails, however, a day of reckoning is at hand. The group of Pawns becomes an over-extended

White enjoys a powerful Pawn storming assault. If it succeeds, all is well . . .

. . . If it fails, this may be the result. White's Pawns will be picked off one by one.

Pawn position. It is itself easy prey, and the men which it should shelter are at the mercy of enemy forces.

The Pawn "Hole"

As a result of unskilled Pawn advances, Pawn barriers are breached and Pawn weaknesses accrue. To a lesser extent, a single bad Pawn move affects the position. If a Pawn advances so that an enemy piece can lodge in front of it or in front of some other Pawn and the enemy piece cannot be driven away by a Pawn, then the Pawn position has been punctured. The puncture is technically called a "hole."

A "hole" is a weakness in the Pawn structure. It is a haven for an enemy piece—an outpost for an enemy attack.

Black has holes at his K4, QB4 and QR4. White should exploit these.

White occupies the hole at his KN6. This is a powerful post for the Rook.

B—Pawn Advantages

PAWNS have many weaknesses and many Pawn structures are faulty. What then may be sought to advantage in building up a Pawn structure?

Pawn Majority

At the beginning of the game, the opposing Pawn structures are perfectly matched. For every White Pawn, there is an equivalent Black Pawn. As the game progresses and exchanges take place, the Pawn position is apt to go out of balance. Pawn majorities may likely be established in different sectors. One side may obtain an extra Pawn in the center, while the other obtains an extra Pawn on the wing. Or one side may obtain an extra Pawn on the wing, while the other side obtains an extra Pawn on the other wing.

The unbalanced Pawn position often injects a new strategic plan into the game. The extra Pawn, whether it is on the wing or in the center, is a constant threat. It is a threat of a potential new Queen, which materializes when the Pawn reaches the eighth rank. While the actual Queening may take place in the endgame, opening play may account for the Pawn majority.

Technically, a Pawn majority exists when the Pawns on one side outnumber the Pawns on the other side. Actually, the majority is impotent if it can be held in check by the Pawn minority.

A mobile Pawn majority is another advantage which may be effected in the opening.

White has a center Pawn majority. Black has a Queen-side Pawn majority. Chances are about even.

Black's King-side Pawn majority is mobile; White's majority on the other wing is fixed. Black should win.

The "Breaks"

Pawn chains perform various functions. They are the first line of fire. They attack and they defend.

In order to break through to the opposing forces, generally the opposing Pawn chain must be broken. Then pieces can

EXAMPLES OF THE "BREAK"

Black enjoys the "break" . . . P-KB4, whenever he is ready. In doing so, he may open the King Bishop file.

White now can "break" with P-QN5, forcing open the Bishop file or weakening Black's Pawn position.

penetrate on the newly opened line—file, rank or diagonal. As a rule, a vulnerable point is selected for the break, and, after due preparation, the break is effected. The ability to force open lines in the opponent's Pawn chain is technically known as the ability to "break." To enjoy the "breaks" is an advantage. In building up opening patterns, it is wise to eye the possible "breaks" in the position.

The Passed Pawn

The most dangerous Pawn on the chessboard is the one which is not impeded in its advance by an opposing Pawn. It is known technically as the "passed Pawn," meaning that it has by-passed all the opposing Pawns. Ergo, it enjoys easy access to the eighth rank, and, in turn, it will burden an opposing piece with the duty of preventing the Pawn from Queening.

Often, in the opening melee, it is possible to obtain a passed Pawn. Such a Pawn adds a definite plus value to the position.

THE INITIATIVE

According to the rules of chess, the first move is arbitrarily bestowed upon White. This seemingly insignificant fact is

White's King Pawn is passed. It will bear constant watching all through the game.

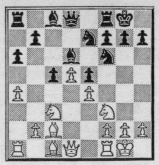

White's Queen Pawn is passed. It has by-passed all of Black's Pawns.

EXAMPLES OF THE INITIATIVE

Despite the symmetrical position, White's first move 1 NxNch gives him a powerful attack. In a critical position (see next), it can even win.

Here the first move is good enough to win the Queen or give mate: 1 N-K7ch, K-R1; 2 BxPch, KxB; 3 Q-N5ch, K-K-R1; 4 Q-B6 mate.

sufficient to give White the initiative. He is first to bring out his men; he is first to control the center. Black, on the other hand, is relegated to the role of defender.

The forces are so evenly balanced that White, with perfect play, can maintain the initiative far into the middle game. White's ambition is to translate the initiative into tangible gain. Black's aim is to reduce White's initiative to a minimum. The conflict is drawn along these lines.

IDEAL OPENING POSITIONS

The ideal position from a practical point of view is more or less of a pipe dream. It can be reached only if the opponent is oblivious of the principles of chess.

All of White's minor pieces and his King Pawn and Queen Pawn bear on the center. White's Rooks can move to the King and Queen files.

Here White's Pawns dominate the center with the assistance of the minor men. White's Bishops bolster any center action.

White's haphazard development gives Black control of the center, easy development, fine prospects—in short, an ideal formation.

There has been no contest in the center. White's Bishops participate in the center action from the wings, while his Pawns occupy the center.

PRACTICAL OPENING PATTERNS

During the last hundred years, patterns of play have evolved. They are called openings. Their names derive from the place or tournament in which they were first played or from the player who originated them or from the chessmaster who popularized them. The patterns are dissimilar even though their objectives are the same.

A discussion of the fundamental patterns, a knowledge of which is essential to the proper understanding of the game, will follow in succeeding chapters.

3

Giuoco Piano

THE Giuoco Piano is the first recorded opening. It is mentioned in the Göttingen Manuscript (1490) and by all the early authors. It dates from the time when Italy was the ruling power in chess.

Belying its name, which means quiet game, the Giuoco Piano currently is spirited and forceful. It grants White latitude for imagination, leading to exciting combinations, and it is full of pitfalls for the unwary. Its distinguishing feature is the development of White's King Bishop to QB4 on his third move. This characteristic move portends attack.

The opening arises as follows:

1 P-K4 . . . .

The initial skirmish is to gain command of the central squares. *1* P-K4 is an attempt to control the central square Q5 and also the square KB5. While KB5 is not as valuable as Q5, it is within the domain of the central squares.

A secondary reason for the advance of the King Pawn is to release the King Bishop and the Queen for future action.

1 . . . .   P-K4

Black's reasons for this move are basically the same as White's. Other moves, leading to other patterns, will be discussed in due time.

2 N-KB3 . . . .

The primary purpose of this move is to put additional pressure on the central squares, in this case the squares K5 and Q4. Eventually, by concerted pressure, White hopes to reach the goal of gaining command of the central squares. Incidentally, the move attacks Black's King Pawn.

2 . . . . N-QB3

While the attack on the King Pawn is incidental to White, it is of prime importance to Black. The loss of even a puny Pawn, as a rule, is of greater value than control of the central squares. That is why Black defends the Pawn. His choice of defense, moreover, is good. For the text move does double duty: it defends the King Pawn and puts pressure on central squares—Black's K4 and Q5.

3 B-B4 . . . .

Again, White eyes the center. The Bishop bears down on Q5. Also, the move does double duty. The most vulnerable square in Black's camp is KB2. That square is adjacent to the King and is defended only by the King. The newly developed Bishop, therefore, not only bears down on the center, but also on the vulnerable square.

The single attack on Black's weak spot, at this stage of the game, is almost insignificant. It may become potent, however, as the game progresses.

3 . . . .   B-B4

Black follows suit for the same reason.

At this juncture, there are many ways of continuing—active and passive. For years, the passive way was in vogue. This consisted of emphasizing development, without any particular goal. White would bring out his Queen Knight to B3, play his Pawn to Q3 and castle; Black would do likewise. The resultant symmetrical position would tend towards a draw. Currently, White's treatment of the opening is different. He attempts to capture the center by force.

4 P-B3 . . . .

An effective way of dominating the center is by doing so with Pawns. The text move is preparatory to the advance of the Queen Pawn.

4 . . . .   N-B3

Black cannot afford to permit the execution of White's plan without adequate countermeasures. His choice is to attack White's King Pawn. This places obstacles in White's path. For the unguarded King Pawn requires attention.

Black's method of meeting White's threat to obtain control

of the center is technically known as the counter-attack. An alternative line is *4 . . . Q-K2*. Then, if White continues with 5 P-Q4, Black does not capture, but retreats his Bishop to N3. Black's King Pawn is defended by Knight and Queen, and White cannot compel Black to exchange Pawns. In the event of the exchange, Black has no King Pawn, and White will remain with King and Queen Pawns. The extra center Pawn in White's favor will result in White's domination of the center.

The *4 . . . Q-K2* line of play may well be called the "hold the line" defense. In practice, however, it has been found deficient. For Black runs out of good moves, sooner or later, and must bide his time awaiting the moment when White will strike.

5 **P-Q4** . . . .

According to plan. White disregards the attack on his King Pawn as he is attacking Black's King Pawn with a preponderance of force.

5 . . . . **PxP**

More or less forced. If, for example, *5 . . . B-N3; 6 PxP, KNxP; 7 Q-Q5* and, since White threatens checkmate as well as the Black Knight, he must win a piece. Nor will *5 . . . B-Q3* do as it impedes Black's development. Black's Queen Bishop will be unable to get out for some time.

6 **PxP** . . . .

Again, according to plan. White wishes to dominate the central squares with Pawns. Observe that 6 NxP would be the complete negation of White's plan.

6 . . . . **B-N5ch**

This foreseen, tempo-gaining device is the saving clause. If the Bishop were to retreat to N3 or K2, White could completely rout the Black forces by advancing P-Q5, followed by P-K5.

7 **N-B3** . . . .

The text move has the earmarks of speculation, for it involves material sacrifice. One Pawn goes immediately, another will follow on the subsequent move, and in the main line there is a trap baited with a Rook. Experience, however, proves this to be the best plan at White's command. For he obtains excellent attacking chances.

Instead, White can play safe with 8 B-Q2. Then, after 8 . . . BxBch; 9 QNxB, White's King Pawn is defended. Black, however, will continue with 9 . . . P-Q4, for, after 10 PxP, KNxP, White will remain with an isolated Queen Pawn. True, White commands more of the central squares than Black. But his isolated Pawn is a liability which does not add up to his asset.

7 . . . . NxKP

The capture of the King Pawn engenders a certain amount of risk for both sides! Black leaves himself open to attack, and White suffers from the material loss of the Pawn. Consequently, White will endeavor to capitalize his initiative, and Black will strive for consolidation.

Failure to capture the Pawn, on the other hand, would be an error of judgment. For then White would have achieved his goal—command of the center—at no cost.

Nor would it be wise for Black to cede the center in the hope of battering it down with 7 . . . P-Q4. This move has been tried and found wanting.   (See CHESS MOVIE, page 43,) It is only by incisive play that White refutes 7 . . . P-Q4. This is traceable to the early opening of the King file for White's attack.

8 O-O . . . .

In order to unpin the Queen Knight, secure the White King from molestation and mobilize the White King Rook for action, possibly on the open King file.

8 . . . . NxN

With a Pawn plus and the attacking chances favoring White, Black's best chance is to cut down the forces to reduce the impact of any brewing attack.

8 . . . BxN has been tried on the same grounds and found distasteful. This move leaves open the spectacular counter stroke 9 P-Q5, known as the Moeller Attack. The resultant position is perilous for both sides. (*See* CHESS MOVIE, *page 46*,)

9 PxN   . . . .

9 . . . .   P-Q4!

An important interpolation. The counter-attack on White's Bishop gives Black the opportunity to open new lines for rapid development. Since Black's uncastled King will be in the crossfire of White's ready batteries, Black must utilize every available means to free his forces for defense.

Alternatives are dangerous for Black. For instance, if 9 . . . BxP, White obtains the better game as follows: *10* B-R3!, N-K2; *11* Q-N3, P-Q4; *12* QxB, PxB; *13* KR-K1, B-K3; *14* BxN, KxB; *15* P-Q5, QxP; *16* QR-Q1 with an overwhelming attack. E.g., *16* . . . Q-QB4; *17* R-K5, Q-N3; *18* RxBch!, QxR; *19* R-K1 and wins.

In this line, if—instead of *10* . . . N-K2—Black plays *10* . . . P-Q4, there follows: *11* B-N5, BxR; *12* R-K1ch, B-K3; *13* Q-R4, R-QN1; *14* N-K5, Q-B1; *15* BxNch, PxB; *16* QxPch, K-Q1; *17* NxPch, BxN; *18* B-K7 mate.

It is impossible within the scope of this work to cover the reasons behind the moves in the sub- and sub-sub-variations. Nonetheless, the learner can turn what seems like a fault into a virtue. By experimenting at each stumbling block, the learner will familiarize himself with the possibilities of the position. At the same time, he will obtain a firm grasp of what is involved.

For instance, in the above variation (see position after 9 PxN and play . . . BxP; *10* B-R3), what happens if Black plays *10* . . . BxR, instead of *10* . . . N-K2? After all, a Rook is more valuable than a Bishop. The answer comes rapidly. White will continue with *11* R-K1*ch*, compelling Black to interpose . . . N-K2. White will follow up *12* BxN, QxB; *13* RxQ*ch*, KxR; *14* QxB and should win.

Or, in the same variation, after *10* . . . N-K2; *11* Q-N3, if Black captures *11* . . . BxR, how shall White proceed? The answer here is less obvious. But it is not difficult. White plays *12* BxP*ch*, K-B1; *13* R-K1, P-Q3; *14* N-N5. In doing so, White threatens to retreat his Bishop to KN6 or KR5 and menace mate at B7. Black has no valid defense.

There is still another logical-looking move for Black at his 9th turn. (See position after 9 PxN.) It is 9 . . . B-K2. At first sight, this seems to consolidate Black's position and permits him to retain the extra Pawn—just what Black is seeking. Sharp play on the part of White, however, will make Black's task difficult. E.g., 9 . . . B-K2; *10* P-Q5, N-N1; *11* P-Q6, PxP; *12* BxP*ch*, KxB; *13* Q-Q5*ch*, K-B1; *14* N-N5, Q-K1; *15* R-K1, and White's positional superiority makes Black's material plus of no consequence.

Observe the lack of mobility of the Black forces. The entire Queen-side is hemmed in. Of course, the onus rests upon White to capitalize quickly on his plus, before Black develops. But it can be done. With correct play, the Black King should fall a target to White's trained guns. Or failing that, Black will be compelled to part with his ill-gotten gains and more.

10 **PxB**   . . . .

Now, if White moves his Bishop, Black is able to consolidate and retain the extra Pawn.

$$10 \ldots \ldots \quad \textbf{PxB}$$
$$11 \ \textbf{R-K1ch} \ldots \ldots$$

A Pawn behind, White has compensation in his pressure on the opposing King. He must utilize this to the full.

$$11 \ldots \ldots \quad \textbf{N-K2}$$

11 . . . B-K3; 12 P-Q5 wins a piece.

$$12 \ \textbf{P-N5!} \ldots \ldots$$

Threatening *13* B-R3.

Another way is *12* Q-K2, B-K3; *13* B-N5, Q-Q4; *14* BxN, KxB; *15* Q-B2. White's compensation for his Pawn minus is Black's awkward King position. While this line is also in the spirit of the opening, exacting play is required of both sides. The chances are about even.

$$12 \ldots \ldots \quad \textbf{O-O}$$

To release the annoying pin.

$$13 \ \textbf{B-R3} \qquad \textbf{R-K1}$$
$$14 \ \textbf{Q-B2} \ldots \ldots$$

White must recover his Pawn. *14 . . .* B-K3 is met by *15* N-N5, threatening mate and the exchange of the Bishop which guards the Pawn. White will be saddled with an isolated Queen Pawn as against which his superior development and greater command of terrain are compensation. With correct play, the outcome is likely a draw.

Conclusions

Since the Giuoco Piano is a wild and woolly game, with tactical threats and combinations predominating, it should appeal to the type of player whose imagination occasionally runs rampant.

Despite its age, the Giuoco still lends itself to current refinements. Black's 9th move, for instance, is a recent innovation, superseding another move which was long considered best and which now stands refuted.

The following two CHESS MOVIES are typical examples of lines in the *Giuoco Piano*.

Chess Movie
UNLUCKY SEVEN

Rᴇᴛʀɪʙᴜᴛɪᴏɴ in chess follows closely upon the heels of omission. Below, however, von Bardeleben (Black) wears seven-league boots; his imperceptible error on move seven noticeably remains unpunished for many moves. Inevitable fate and one-time world champion, W. Steinitz (White), finally catch up with a classic refutation, for which Steinitz obtained the brilliancy prize at Hastings, 1895.

1 The coming scene is the Giuoco Piano; the synopsis: 1 P-K4, P-K4; 2 N-KB3, N-QB3; 3 B-B4, B-B4; 4 P-B3, N-B3; 5 P-Q4, PxP; 6 PxP, B-N5ch; 7 N-B3, P-Q4. By vigorous prosecution of the initiative, and with a long bead on the Black monarch, Steinitz dooms Black's defense.

2 There follows 8 PxP, KNxP; 9 O-O, B-K3, arriving at the next position. Superficially, Black is well off. White's isolated Queen Pawn is a handicap, while Black's development is sound and his Pawn chain is solid. All is not what it seems. A few deft strokes and Steinitz is in command.

3 First comes *10* B-KN5, molesting the Queen. Bardeleben parries with *10 . . .* B-K2. Then follows a general exchange: *11* BxN, B/3xB; *12* NxB, QxN. The strategical plan is mysterious. If Steinitz wishes to attack, he must maintain his forces. But, instead, he is swapping down!

4 Violation upon violation: Steinitz continues to swap. There follows *13* BxB, NxB. In another move, Black will castle and hammer away at White's weak, isolated Pawn. But ho! the master has something up his sleeve. He plays *14* R-K1, pinning the Black Knight against its own King.

5 There are pins and pins. This pin appears to be a piddling pin. Bardeleben will snap it with ease. He plays *14 . . .* P-KB3, creating an exit for his King. By *15* Q-K2, however, Steinitz piles upon the pinned piece. Bardeleben defends with *. . .* Q-Q2, and there follows: *16* QR-B1, P-B3.

6 Bardeleben has built a barrier. Steinitz crashes through with *17* P-Q5. There follows *17 . . .* PxP; *18* N-Q4, K-B2; *19* N-K6. A Knight at K6 is like a bone in the throat, says Steinitz. Now he must prove it. He has already invested a Pawn in his principles! A Pawn from Steinitz is rarer than rubies!

7 The threat is Rook to the seventh rank. A "pig on the seventh" can make life miserable. So Bardeleben parries with *19 . . . KR-QB1*. Now follows *20 Q-N4*. The threat is QxPch with mate to follow. White also focuses his attention on the Black Queen which is unguarded.

8 Bardeleben parries with *20 . . . P-KN3*. Steinitz withdraws *21 N-N5ch*, exposing Black's Queen to jeopardy. The King comes to the aid of the beleaguered lady with *. . . K-K1*. The moment is tense as Bardeleben awaits the next thrust. It is no thrust; it is a meat axe. *22 RxNch* is the move.

9 Bardeleben moves *22 . . . K-B1*. He can't play *. . . QxR* because of RxRch. A merry chase ensues: *23 R-B7ch, K-N1; 24 R-N7ch, K-R1; 25 RxPch*. All the time, Black's Queen is immune. For if ever RxQ, Black replies *. . . RxRch* with mate to follow. Bardeleben now bows out of the picture.

10 The finale would be *25 . . . K-N1; 26 R-N7ch, K-R1* when a mate in 9 ensues: *27 Q-R4ch, KxR; 28 Q-R7ch, K-B1; 29 Q-R8ch, K-K2; 30 Q-N7ch, K-K1; 31 Q-N8ch, K-K2; 32 Q-B7ch, K-Q1; 33 Q-B8ch, Q-K1; 34 N-B7ch, K-Q2; 35 Q-Q6 mate*. Small wonder Steinitz was world champion 27 years.

♚ ♛ ♙♙♙♙♙♙♙♙♙♙♙♙♙♙♙♙ ♛ ♚

Chess Movie
SECOND FEATURE: MURDER AT K7

Position is everything on the chessboard. Forces entering the charmed circle of an engaging action are relatively more important at the moment than powerful pieces on the side-lines. Such is the course of the following game: The first engaging action is the last! The players? . . . merely White and Black. Their identity is lost in anonymity. The game opens with *1* P-K4, P-K4; *2* N-KB3, N-QB3; *3* B-B4, B-B4; *4* P-B3, N-B3. (*See diagram No. 1.*)

1 The game continues: 5 P-Q4, PxP; *6* PxP, B-N5*ch;* 7 N-B3, NxKP; 8 O-O, BxN; *9* P-Q5! This launches into a variation which is known as the Moeller Attack. From the beginning, it is clear this is a wild and woolly match between position and material.

2 Already a piece plus, Black is ready for punishment. Material salves abuse. He plays 9 . . . N-K4, counter-attacking the White Bishop. The game continues *10* PxB, NxB; *11* Q-Q4. White's Queen attacks in all directions—both Knights and the Knight Pawn are targets.

3 Safety first is not Black's code. He might as well be hanged for a Knight as well as for a Pawn. So he retreats *11 . . . N/B5-Q3.* White captures *12 QxNP*, attacking the Rook. And Black parries: *12 . . . Q-B3.* So far, so good. Black retains the loot.

4 Now White is accommodating. A piece behind, he swaps Queens: *13 QxQ, NxQ.* With Queens off the board and the mating attacks cut to a minimum, the extra piece looms large in the reckoning. But White is just beginning to fight. *14 R-K1ch* is the move.

5 Black plays *14 . . . K-B1.* He holds on to everything. He does not wish to interpose and return a Knight. The onus of forcing the issue rests with White. He draws the mating net tight about the Black monarch, before Black's reserves come out. *15 B-R6ch, K-N1; 16 R-K5,* menacing mate.

6 Black staves off mate by *15 . . . N/B3-K5.* White continues *16 QR-K1,* meaning to capture the Knight. And Black defends with *. . . P-KB4.* Now White covers all the exits with *17 R-K7.* There follows: *17 . . . P-N3; 18 N-R4, B-N2; 19 P-B3.* The Knight must flee. But where?

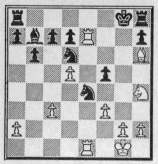

7 First Black counters with *19 . . . N-B2.* Attacking White's Bishop, he hopes to break up the intrusion. But White is adamant. The Bishop will not move. *20 NxP* is the move. All of White's men are in the fray. And Black dare not pare down. If he tries, he loses material but White keeps position.

8 Retreat is in order, *20 . . . N/5-Q3* follows. Still everything is intact. Maybe White's onslaught is spent. Maybe now the extra piece will tell . . . Maybe . . . But Black is day-dreaming. He is rudely awakened. The punishment will fit his crimes in overflowing measure.

9 White crashes through with *21 R-K8ch.* Can such things be and overcome us? What of all the principles of chess? Can Rooks be flaunted defiantly in the face of overpowering material odds? . . . Well, all is well that ends well. For the right side, indeed, it is spectacularly so!

10 Now comes the denouement. *21 . . . RxR; 22 RxRch, NxR; 23 N-K7 mate!* What a picture! Black is a Rook and Knight ahead—a lot of useless wood strewn about the beheaded King. Moral: Material isn't everything in chess. Development is important—on the right squares.

4

Ruy Lopez

T HE Ruy Lopez was named after a Spanish clergyman, Ruy Lopez of Safra, in Estramadura. About the middle of the sixteenth century, he edited a systematic work of one hundred and fifty pages, which presented the results of research into the openings.

First noticed by the writer of the Göttingen Ms. (1490) and later analyzed by other authors, including Lopez, the opening was seldom adopted in actual play until the middle of the last century. Credit for discovering its potency is due the Russian analyst, Jaenisch, who probed its possibilities during the years 1842–68.

White's third move, 3 B-N5, characterizes the Lopez. It is a move which attacks an adverse piece that is bearing on the center squares. Hence it exerts direct pressure on the center in an indirect manner.

The patterns which evolve from this opening are close and positional in the budding period. When in full bloom, however, there is a tendency towards wide-open play.

The opening arises as follows:

1 P-K4   P-K4   2 N-KB3 N-QB3
3 B-N5 . . . .

White's last move is the signal for the opening strategical skirmish for control of the center. Pressure on Black's Knight, which defends its King Pawn, is the motivating reason.

The development of White's King Knight and King Bishop paves the way for early King-side castling. In turn, the King Rook may soon join the fray.

3 . . . . P-QR3

This move is the basis of Black's future defensive formation. Since he may not have the opportunity to do so later on, Black drives White's Bishop at once.

Alternatives are 3 . . . N-B3, 3 . . . B-B4 and 3 . . . N-Q5. These defenses are not in vogue today.

4 B-R4 . . . .

White retreats. If 4 BxN, QPxB; 5 NxP, Q-Q5! recovers the Pawn because of the simultaneous attack on Knight and Pawn.

Since White cannot win a Pawn by the exchange, there is no point to swapping a Bishop for a Knight.

It is to be noted that the reason White cannot win a Pawn is that his own King Pawn is unprotected. The retreat of the Bishop consequently is a marking-time maneuver, with a view to exchanging at a more propitious moment, when White's King Pawn is defended.

4 . . . . N-B3

Since White cannot win a Pawn by BxN, followed by NxP, Black has nothing to fear. He proceeds with his own development, attacking White's center Pawn.

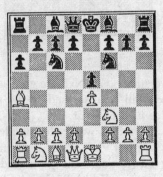

5 O-O! . . . .

Usually, when a Pawn is attacked, it should be defended. Here, for example, White's King Pawn is attacked, and it might be defended by 5 P-Q3 or 5 N-B3. These moves, in fact, are alternatives to the text. Because of tactical reasons, however, which will soon become apparent, White need not defend the Pawn at this moment. And by this omission, White gains time to build up a strong formation which he has in mind.

The point becomes clearer when White's plan is revealed. He intends to establish a Pawn center by playing P-B3, followed by P-Q4. If he defends his King Pawn by playing 5 N-B3, he pre-empts the square QB3 for the Knight and consequently cannot use it for P-B3. If he defends the Pawn with

5 P-Q3, he must abandon the idea of playing P-Q4 later. Else, he loses time by advancing his Pawn to Q4 in two moves, instead of one. Any immediate defense of the King Pawn has certain drawbacks.

5 . . . .   **B-K2**

The text move and 5 . . . NxP are good alternatives at this point. 5 . . . NxP will be discussed in the next chapter. For the present, suffice it to say that, if 5 . . . NxP, White can recover the Pawn in various ways, the simplest being 6 R-K1.

From Black's point of view, it can be seen that the removal of White's King Pawn clears the path leading to the Black King. If the Pawn goes, a White Rook at K1 faces the opposing monarch. And this spells danger. It is with this in mind, that Black makes the text move.

The Bishop at K2 serves to shield the King from a subsequent attack on the King file. The move really is anticipatory. Since the danger is lessened, Black is in a better position to threaten to capture the King Pawn.

Incidentally, other moves with the Bishop will not do as well. For instance, 5 . . . B-Q3 is disadvantageous as the Bishop on Q3 blocks the advance of Black's Queen Pawn. The immobility of the Queen Pawn, in turn, ties up Black's entire Queen-side. 5 . . . B-B4 fails because White can play 6 NxP! Then, if . . . NxN; 7 P-Q4 and White recovers the piece and holds greater control of the central squares. 5 . . . B-N5 will not do, as White counters with the move he intends to make in any event—P-B3. Then the Bishop has to retreat and White gains his goal at Black's expense.

6 R-K1   . . . .

White defends the King Pawn. Now it is inadvisable to grant Black the option of capturing the Pawn.

6 . . . . P-QN4

Since White's King Pawn is defended, the threat of 7 BxN, QPxB; 8 NxP, gaining a Pawn, is real. Observe that 8 . . . Q-Q5 in this instance will not retrieve the Pawn. That is why Black destroys the threat by driving the Bishop.

7 B-N3   P-Q3

Black's last move has a threefold purpose: (*1*) it defends the King Pawn; (*2*) it permits the development of the Queen Bishop along its normal diagonal; (*3*) it institutes the minor threat of 8 . . . N-QR4, followed by 9 . . . NxB, gaining a Bishop for a Knight.

8 P-B3   . . . .

White's move has a twofold purpose: (*1*) it creates an exit for the Bishop, in the event it is attacked by the adverse Knight; (*2*) it prepares for the establishment of a Pawn center, with the Queen Bishop Pawn serving as a prop.

8 . . . . N-QR4

At first sight, this appears to be a purposeless move. The Knight moves out on a limb, merely to attack a Bishop, which will retreat. Closer examination will not reveal the purpose of the move. Only a knowledge of what Black has in mind will clarify the maneuver.

Black is following a preconceived plan. White's plan is to advance his Pawn to Q4, put pressure on Black's King Pawn and compel Black to exchange Pawns. Then White recaptures with the Bishop Pawn. The disappearance of Black's King Pawn, in effect, will be tantamount to the surrender of the center to White.

Black's plan is a parry to White's. He moves the Knight to clear the path of his Queen Bishop Pawn. He aims for a Pawn formation of his own in which the Queen Bishop Pawn plays an important part—in challenging or staying White's ambition to take over the center.

Since the opening has been played time and again, the best plans of both contestants are known to each other. Each side, therefore, is in position to anticipate and counter the other's ideas in the most effective manner.

9 B-B2 . . . .

The Bishop retreats, even at the expense of a move. For a Bishop is stronger than a Knight, and White wishes to avoid the exchange.

9 . . . .   P-B4

This is the reason for Black's 8th move. With Black's Knight at QB3, the Bishop Pawn was fixed.

Now, when, as and if White plays P-Q4, Black still exerts as much pressure on White's center as White on Black's. Moreover, Black's square QB2 is vacated and Black's Queen can occupy it to defend the King Pawn—again, when, as and if it is attacked.

Black's Queen-side Pawn structure is an effective one, known commonly as the Tchigorin formation.

All this delicate maneuvering is to balance the scale as far as the center is concerned.

10 P-Q4 . . . .

Actively striking at the center. The passive line, 10 P-Q3, also has much in its favor and will be discussed in another chapter.

10 . . . . Q-B2

Defending the King Pawn, which is doubly attacked. Note that this is possible only because of Black's 9th, which was preparatory to the text.

The exchange of Pawns: 10 . . . KPxP; 11 PxP, PxP; 12 NxP would be the surrender of the center to White. Moreover, Black would remain with an isolated and backward Queen Pawn.

Even the exchange of one Pawn in the center would benefit White. Thus, if 10 . . . BPxP; 11 PxP, the resulting open Queen Bishop file eventually would accrue to White. Or, if 10 . . . KPxP; 11 PxP leaves White in control of the center with good prospects for attack because of the added possibility of an eventual P-K5.

11 P-KR3 . . . .

The move P-KR3, as a general rule, does more harm than good. In this case, for example, it weakens White's King-side flank to a minor extent. The weakness, however, in this instance, is more than offset by the gain in other directions. Here,

the Pawn at R3 prevents Black from pinning White's King Knight with . . . B-N5. The pin would not be fatal for White, but it would mitigate the pressure which the White Knight exerts in the center.

In addition, the Pawn at R3 serves as a prop for an eventual P-KN4 and an all-out advance of the King-side Pawns against the opposing King—when the position calls for it.

11 . . . .   O-O

The skirmish to gain control of the center is a stand off; Black's defense has not yielded to White's pressure.

12 QN-Q2 . . . .

Such a Knight move is normally condemned by the layman. For the Knight at Q2 interferes with the development of the

Queen Bishop. The interference, however, is only temporary. In one move, the Knight can clear the path.

More important is its purpose. What does it portend? . . . It is the beginning of a maneuver to transfer the Knight to the King-side of the board. Why the King-side? . . . Because White is making plans to institute a King-side attack. In order to do this, he must bring forces within the range of the oppos-ing King.

12 . . . . N-B3

So long as the tension exists in the center, it is difficult for either side to undertake a constructive plan on the wings. Since White is contemplating a King-side assault, Black piles on the pressure in the center—to keep White employed in that sector.

13 P-Q5 . . . .

As there is no way for White to put additional pressure on Black's center and compel Black to exchange Pawns, White ends the tension in the center by the advance of the Pawn. This relieves White of the need to guard the center and frees him for operating on the wing. In this instance, it is the King's wing in which White is interested.

Of course, with the end of the center tension, Black is also free to operate in other sectors.

13 . . . . N-Q1

A unique move which has all the superficial appearances of inanity. From Q1, the Knight cannot go the K3 or back to B3. Yet at QN2, it has little bearing on the position. Moreover, it interferes now with the communications between Black's other forces.

Despite appearances, *13 . . .* N-Q1 is a good move. It is the first step in the plan to build up a defense against White's contemplated assault on the Black King. Follow the Knight meanderings to its final destination to observe what Black has in mind.

14 N-B1 . . . .

Primarily to maneuver the Knight to the King-side; secondarily to clear the path of the Bishop.

14 . . . .   N-K1

This is another unique move in Black's concealed plan of defense. Its immediate purpose is to threaten a break by the advance *15 . . .* P-KB4. Its long-term purpose will become clear when the final pattern of Black's defense is woven.

15 P-KN4 . . . .

This advance forestalls Black's intended break. That, however, is not the main purpose of the move. As a matter of strategy, it is important to provoke weaknesses in the enemy camp.

To do so by a Pawn advance is the least expensive way. In an
assault which stands a fair chance of success, Pawns are ex-
pendable. Thus, the Pawns advance with a view to provoking
weaknesses or opening gaps, and the major pieces will follow,
intent upon exploitation.

True, White's Pawn advance is double-edged. Any Pawn
advance is inherently weak. Here, the weakness is relatively
unimportant at this stage of the game, while there is a respecta-
ble attack brewing. So long as the attack is significant, the
weakness will not show up. Should the attack fail, however,
there is danger that White's weaknesses will boomerang. But
such a possibility, if it does arise, will turn up only at a much
later stage of the game.

15 . . . . P-N3

With a dual purpose. The immediate reason for the move is
to create a square at KN2 for the King Knight, where it will
serve in a defensive capacity. The long-term purpose is to keep
an eye on the possible break . . . P-B4, should the opportunity
present itself.

16 N-N3 . . . .

Attaining the object of the Knight maneuver, which was to
bring the Knight into the vicinity of the adverse King.

16 . . . . P-B3

To vacate the square . . . KB2 so that the Knight on Q1 can move up for defense. The secret of Black's *13 . . . N-Q1* is out.

17 K-R2 . . . .

To clear the King Knight file for future occupation by White's Rooks—all part and parcel of a grand attacking plan.

17 . . . . N-B2

Building a defensive barrier, in anticipation of the attack.

18 R-KN1 . . . .

Despite the presence of White and Black Pawns on the King Knight file, the Rook bears down, indirectly, upon the Black Monarch. White is looking ahead to the time when the Pawns may be cleared off the file.

18 . . . . K-R1

To get out of the line of fire of the adverse Rook.

19 B-K3 . . . .

This assists in clearing the first rank so as to enable the Queen Rook to join the King-side assault.

19 . . . . N-N2

Consolidating the defensive barrier. The final destinations of the Black Knights in the opening are achieved.

20 Q-Q2 . . . .

Completely clearing the way for the Queen Rook to join the fray. White also eyes B-R6 as a possibility.

20 . . . . B-Q2

To clear the last rank so as to enable both Black Rooks to cooperate.

21 R-KN2 . . . .

Vacating KN1 for the Queen Rook.

21 . . . . R-KN1

Neutralizing the indirect pressure on the King Knight file.

22 QR-KN1. . . .

Thereby joining the attack in full force. White's last is technically called "doubling the Rooks."

To all intents and appearance, White has the initiative. Black, however, is well poised for defense. With best play, a draw should result.

A cardinal wit summed up the position succinctly with "Black will probably win. White's attacking chances will undoubtedly drive him into a rash action."

Conclusions

Of all the openings beginning with *1* P-K4, the Ruy Lopez offers a longer-lasting initiative to White, with the least amount of speculation.

Current opinion concludes that the patterns evolving from this opening should result in a draw. The onus of best play, however, generally rests with Black, as he is the defender. One misstep in the defense is fatal.

Chess Movie

THE GREAT FALL

ALL the King's horses and all the King's men push Humpty Dumpty (the Black Monarch) right off the wall in this modern version of the great fall. Salo Flohr conducts the White forces with unusual vigor, sacrificing nearly more men than there are on the board! F. Lustig is the victim, and the game was played at Prague in 1928. It opens with *1* P-K4, P-K4; *2* N-KB3, N-QB3; *3* B-N5, P-QR3; *4* B-R4, N-B3 (*see diagram No. 1*).

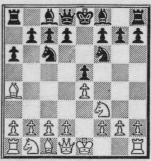

1 The game continues: *5* Q-K2, B-K2; *6* P-B3, P-QN4; *7* B-N3, P-Q3; *8* P-KR3, N-QR4; *9* B-B2, P-B4; *10* P-Q4, Q-B2; *11* O-O, O-O. This makes an illustrative game for the analysis preceding, as the standard line has been reached. The Queen at K2 doesn't alter the *general* pattern.

2 Intent upon a King-side assault, Flohr relaxes the center tension with *12* P-Q5. Lustig counters with a Queen-side advance . . . P-B5, as he underestimates the power of the coming onslaught against his King. Both sides continue their development: *13* B-K3, B-Q2, readying for the next round.

3 Flohr retreats *14* N-K1. He intends to advance his King Bishop Pawn to open the King Bishop file for future operations. Lustig retires . . . N-N2. There follows *15* N-Q2, KR-K1. Lustig has ideas of his own concerning defense. Flohr spikes his Pawn: *16* P-KN4, and Lustig replies *16* . . . P-N3.

4 Now nearly all of the White forces are ready for the coming fracas. There is no reason why they should not all participate. So Flohr advances *17* P-B4, opening the Bishop file. Lustig captures . . . PxP, and Flohr recaptures *18* RxP. Black now returns . . . R-KB1 in order to guard his vital KB2.

5 Flohr retires *19* R-B2, clearing the diagonal for his Queen Bishop, and Lustig replies . . . N-K1. Too late, he wishes to set up the typical Knight barrier. There follows: *20* N/1-B3, N-Q1; *21* QR-KB1, P-B3; *22* B-R6, N-KN2. The stage is neatly set for a penetrating incursion, in the brilliant style.

6 There are many ways of slowly building the attack. There is only one way of reaching the Sable monarch with full force, pronto. It involves the sacrifice of a Pawn for vague returns. As Flohr's good judgment commands, however, he now crashes through with the speculative *23* P-K5.

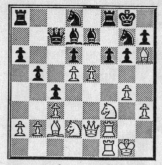

7 With one fell stroke, the White King Bishop aims at the Black monarch, and the White Queen Knight has gained a new base for operations at K4. Lustig takes 23 . . . QPxP, and Flohr moves in: 24 N-K4. Lustig covers with . . . N-B2, and there follows: 25 BxN, KxB. Can Black now survive?

8 Flohr plays 26 N-R4, and Lustig counters with . . . N-Q3. Now Flohr takes a do or die stand: 27 NxBP! and the Black barrier is breached. Lustig accepts the sacrifice by . . . BxN. Flohr hits hard with 28 P-N5. The fur is flying, and it is difficult to keep track of the fast-moving action.

9 Lustig defends with 28 . . . N-K1, and Flohr rains another blow at the ill-fated King: 29 NxP!! Lustig takes . . . PxN, and the action waxes fast and furious: 30 BxP, KxB; 31 Q-K4ch. At long last and at the expense of all of three pieces, the Black monarch is nakedly exposed—to a fatal chill!

10 The King retreats, 31 . . . K-N2, seeking protection, and there follows a peaceful haymaker: 32 Q-R4. Now follows: 32 . . . K-N1; 33 PxB, NxP; 34 Q-N5ch, K-R1; 35 RxN and the well-known spite check . . . Q-B4ch. Flohr simply retires gracefully: 36 K-R2, and Lustig gives up the ghost.

5

Ruy Lopez

THE OPEN DEFENSE

In the main variation of the Ruy Lopez, White maintains the initiative clearly throughout the opening and well into the middle game. Although Black can achieve equality with best play, the onus of perfection rests on him. It is indeed unappetizing for a player to be confronted with a line which, at best and after taxing him to the utmost, grants mere equality. There is, nonetheless, no known method for Black to seize the initiative—bestowed upon White—without incurring certain risks.

There is, however, an active line for Black. This defense grants him a considerable measure of counterplay at the expense of security of position. For the player who prefers the rough and tumble way, the active, or so-called open, defense is the answer.

This defense arises as follows:

1 P-K4	P-K4		*3* B-N5	P-QR3
2 N-KB3	N-QB3		*4* B-R4	N-B3
	5 O-O	NxP		

By capturing the King Pawn, Black exposes his King Knight as a target and opens lines leading to his King. Since White must devote his efforts to recovering the Pawn and maintaining his initiative, Black enjoys some leeway.

6 P-Q4 . . . .

This move offers White the best chance of reaching both his objectives—the recovery of the Pawn and the retention of his initiative.

6 R-K1 also recovers the Pawn. For there is no good way for Black to retain it. Thus, if *6* . . . P-Q4; 7 NxP. Or, if *6* . . . N-B4; 7 NxP.

The text move, however, is superior to *6* R-K1; for, on *6* . . . N-B4; 7 NxP, B-K2, White is compelled to part with one of his Bishops for a Knight, without getting any compensation in return.

6 . . . . P-QN4

Black wishes to play . . . P-Q4. He can not do so at once; for, after *6* . . . P-Q4; *7* NxP, Black is virtually forced to play *7* . . . B-Q2 or place his pieces on awkward posts. A rather subtle combination then follows: e.g., *6* . . . P-Q4; *7* NxP, B-Q2; *8* NxP! KxN; *9* Q-R5*ch*, K-K3; *10* N-B3, and White's onslaught is overwhelming.*

Thus, by first driving the Bishop, Black is able to follow with . . . P-Q4 as his Queen Knight will not be pinned.

7 **B-N3**   **P-Q4**

As per plan.

8 **PxP**   . . . .

The text move is superior to *8* NxP on tactical and strategical grounds. If *8* NxP, for example, the continuation is *8* . . . NxN; *9* PxN, B-K3. Then the Black Queen Bishop Pawn is free to advance, and Black's Queen-side majority becomes dangerous. Furthermore, since White is contemplating an eventual King-side assault, he should avoid any unprofitable exchanges. Attack is based on force, and consequently White should retain his forces.

8 . . . .   **B-K3**

Black defends the Queen Pawn. Now he threatens *9* . . . N-B4 to gain a Bishop for a Knight.

9 **P-B3**   . . . .

* Chernev, I., *Winning Chess Traps*, N. Y., McKay, p. 41.

White creates an exit for the Bishop in the event that it is attacked. 9 Q-K2 is an alternative but highly involved line of play. In it, White readily parts with his Bishop, if need be, in return for unmitigated pressure on the Black Queen Pawn. He follows up with R-Q1.

9 . . . .   **B-K2**

Black prepares to castle and to complete his development. 9 . . . B-QB4 is an inferior alternative.

10 **QN-Q2** . . . .

White aims to rid himself of Black's advanced Knight.

10 . . . .   **O-O**

11 **B-B2**   . . . .

White puts pressure on Black's well posted Knight. If instead 11 NxN, PxN; 12 BxB, PxB, White's King Knight must move, and his King Pawn goes by the wayside. Then White achieves mere equality, at best, when naturally he is seeking an advantage.

11 . . . .   P-B4

Black aims to maintain the Knight at K5. Inferior alternatives are: (*a*) 11 . . . NxN; 12 QxN, P-B3; 13 PxP, BxP; 14 N-N5, BxN; 15 QxB, QxQ; 16 BxQ after which the advantage of the two Bishops and the better Pawn structure rests with White; or (*b*) 11 . . . N-B4; 12 N-Q4 (intending P-KB4-5), NxP; 13 Q-R5, N-N3; 14 P-KB4, B-Q2; 15 P-B5, N-R1; 16 P-B6, with an irresistible attack for White. These alternatives arise from actual games.

Observe that, in order to maintain the Knight at K5, Black permits White to have a protected passed Pawn.

At this juncture, Black enjoys freedom of movement. His Pawn formation, however, is full of holes, which in turn jeopardize the security of his position. As yet, however, no sure way of exploiting these defects has been found.

12 N-N3 . . . .

The alternative, 12 PxP *e.p.*, intending to undermine the support of the Knight, appears to favor Black. E.g., 12 PxP *e.p.*, NxP/3; *13* N-N3, B-KN5!; *14* Q-Q3, N-K5; *15* QN-Q4, NxN; *16* NxN, B-Q3, and Black enjoys attacking prospects: *17* N-B6, Q-R5; *18* QxP*ch*, K-R1; *19* P-KN3, NxNP; *20* RPxN, BxP, and it is difficult for White to ward off the onslaught.

12 . . . .   **Q-Q2**

Black permits cooperation between the Rooks on the last rank. Black is resigned to parting with a Bishop for a Knight. For he expects quickly to utilize his Queen-side Pawn majority.

13 **KN-Q4** . . . .

White attacks Black's Queen Bishop and aims to drive Black's well-posted Knight at K5, at the opportune moment.

13 . . . .   **NxN**

If *13* . . . NxKP; *14* R-K1, the threat of *15* P-B3 or *15* NxB, followed by *16* P-B3, is difficult to handle.

14 **NxN**   . . . .

If *14* PxN, in order to retard the advance of Black's Queen Bishop Pawn, the continuation might be *14* . . . P-QR4; *15* P-B3, P-R5, and Black emerges with a plus in position. For his forces are better posted.

14 . . . .   **P-B4**

Black sets the Pawn majority immediately in motion.

15 N-K2   . . . .

15 NxB gives White the two Bishops. Since Black's Pawns are mobile, however, and White's King Pawn is fixed, the advantage of the two Bishops is dubious. For Knights show at their best in fixed Pawn positions.

The retreat of the Knight is mainly to retain resiliency in the position. The Knight can maneuver to a better post.

15 . . . . QR-Q1

Black reinforces the Queen Pawn, one of the weak spots in the position, and also prepares its advance.

16 N-B4   . . . .

16 . . . . Q-B3

The impetuous advance of either the Queen Pawn or the Queen Bishop Pawn opens lines which White may utilize. For example, if *16* . . . P-B5, *17* B-K3 and Black's Queen Pawn remains backward. Or, if *16* . . . P-Q5; *17* PxP, PxP; *18* NxB, QxN; *19* B-N3 and White wins.

17 Q-R5   . . . .

White threatens to win a piece by *18* NxB, followed by *19* P-B3.

17 . . . . B-B1

Black avoids the threat.

18 P-QR4 . . . .

White seeks to open the Rook file or to disrupt Black's Queen-side Pawn formation.

18 . . . .   P-N5
19 PxP   . . . .

White breaks up Black's chain of Pawns.

19 . . . .   PxP

The position is about even. If any side is to be preferred, it is White's—his passed Pawn can be supported but Black's is isolated.

This variation is from the first game of the match, Bogolyubov vs. Euwe, 1928. The game with Euwe as Black continued:

20	Q-K2	N-B4	27 QR-Q1	P-R3
21	B-K3	P-QR4	28 P-R4	Q-K2
22	BxN	QxB	29 R-Q4	P-N4
23	B-N3	B-N4	30 PxP	PxP
24	Q-B3	BxN	31 Q-Q2	R-Q2
25	QxB	K-R1	32 R-Q1	P-B5
26	KR-K1	B-K3	33 Q-K2	P-B6
	34 Q-K3	Q-R2		

FINAL POSITION

After 35 BxP, BxB; 36 RxB, RxR; 37 RxR, Q-N8*ch;* 38 K-R2, Q-R2*ch* and Black gets a perpetual as 39 K-N3 is mere suicide.

Conclusions

In the Open Defense to the Ruy Lopez, the initiative which Black gains more than offsets his chronically weak Pawn structure. Up to the present, moreover, no sure way has been found of exploiting Black's weaknesses.

Chess Movie

ATTACK ON THE GUARD

THERE comes a time to strike in almost every game, and, having come, moves on. This fleeting moment may mean oblivion or immortality! At Vilna, in 1912, the mighty Akiba Rubinstein (Black) thus penetrated Alekhine's position by a deft sacrifice of the exchange. *1* P-K4, P-K4; *2* N-KB3, N-QB3; *3* B-N5, P-QR3; *4* B-R4, N-B3; *5* O-O, NxP (*see diagram No. 1*).

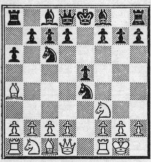 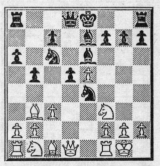

1 Then follow the usual moves of the Open Defense of the Ruy Lopez: *6* P-Q4, P-QN4; *7* B-N3, P-Q4; *8* PxP, B-K3; *9* P-B3, B-K2, arriving at diagram 2. Alekhine versus Rubinstein! Their names will forever be inscribed on Caissa's banner. Both players are alert to exploit small advantages.

2 The game continues: *10* QN-Q2, N-B4, reaching diagram 3. The great Akiba in fighting spirit has experience and reputation on his side. Twenty-one-year-old Alekhine has yet to prove himself, and the speculative text move takes him by surprise. His position, however, is solid, and a real fight ensues.

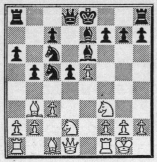

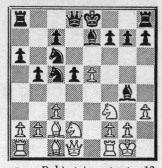

3 Alekhine retreats *11 B-B2* to preserve his Bishop. Rubinstein plays *11 . . . B-N5*, pinning White's King Knight and vacating his K3 square for occupation by his King Knight. Alekhine "puts the question" to the Bishop by *12 P-KR3*. The tempo of the game is rapid. The opening sparring is over.

4 Rubinstein retreats *12 . . . B-R4* and Alekhine answers *13 Q-K1*, breaking the annoying pin. Rubinstein follows with *13 . . . N-K3*, focusing on White's King position. Somehow the initiative has been transferred to Black. The slight weakness of his Pawn formation now assumes a minor role.

5 Alekhine withdraws *14 N-R2*, preparing the advance of his Kingside Pawn majority. Rubinstein parries *14 . . . B-N3*. Alekhine exchanges *15 BxB*. Capture towards the center is a good rule of thumb. Rubinstein, however, does not play with his thumbs. He plays *15 . . . BPxP* to open the Bishop file.

6 With his King-side Pawn roller stymied, Alekhine continues with *16 N-N3*. His opponent counters: *. . . P-KN4*. He checks any ideas of a White Pawn advance on the Kingside. Alekhine develops *17 B-K3*, and there follows: *17 . . . O-O*; *18 N-KB3, Q-Q2*; *19 Q-Q2*, and the critical story is told below.

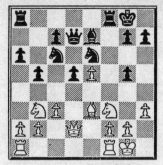

7 Strategically, Black has an uphill battle. White has a passed Pawn and Black's Pawn formation is disrupted. Tactically, there is another story. What does it matter if a Pawn is misplaced, so long as the opposing King is the target? Now *19 . . . RxN!* breaches the defense.

8 Alekhine captures *20 PxR* and then Rubinstein rejoins with *. . . NxP*, threatening a discombobulating check. Now Alekhine defends with *21 Q-K2,* and Rubinstein puts on the heat with *21 . . . R-KB1.* Again Alekhine defends: *22 N-Q2.* And Rubinstein maneuvers *22 . . . N-N3,* eyeing KB5.

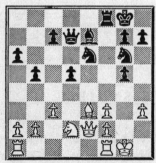

9 Alekhine plays *23 KR-K1,* vacating KB1 for defensive purposes. Rubinstein fires *23 . . . B-Q3,* aiming at White's King. White's ill-fated defenses are beyond repair. Feebly, he tries *24 P-KB4.* Now *24 . . . N/K3xP* penetrates. White retreats *25 Q-B1,* and Black slashes out with *25 . . . Nx Pch.*

10 Black is on the rampage. There follows: *26 K-R1, P-KN5; 27 Q-K2, Q-B4.* With the dire threat of *28 . . . Q-R4* staring him in the face, and with nothing to do about it, Alekhine resigns, without further play. Of such stuff is a reputation made.

Viva Akiba!

6

Ruy Lopez

THE STEINITZ SYSTEM

In the main variation of the Ruy Lopez, White attempts to seize immediate control of the center, before undertaking action on the wing. Another line with equally good prospects for White begins in a more passive manner. White makes no effort to gain the center. Instead, he develops peacefully and soundly. The pacific development, however, is only a front for White's real intentions. All the while, White bides his time and appraises the opportunity to seize the center or to institute an attack against the opposing King.

This line arises as follows:

1 P-K4	P-K4	*3* B-N5	P-QR3
2 N-KB3	N-QB3	*4* B-R4	N-B3

5 P-Q3 . . . .

White directly defends the King Pawn. By not castling now, he reserves the option of castling later on either side, depending on which way the game turns. Or he may remain with his King in the center of the board in some contingencies.

5 . . . . P-Q3

Black defends his King Pawn against the threat of *6* BxN, followed by NxP. In turn, Black now threatens *6* . . . P-QN4; *7* B-N3, N-QR4, followed by the exchange of a Bishop for a Knight.

6 P-B3 . . . .

White creates an exit for the Bishop in the event it is attacked by the adverse Knight. Also, the Queen Bishop Pawn may serve as support for the future advance P-Q4.

6 . . . . B-K2

Black develops the Bishop to permit castling.

7 QN-Q2 . . . .

The beginning of a Knight maneuver (QN-Q2-B1-N3) to the King-side of the board where the Black King will most likely reside. This same maneuver was employed in the earlier variation of the Lopez, discussed in Chapter 4.

7 . . . .   O-O

Whereas White can delay castling, Black finds it more difficult to do so; he cannot undertake a constructive plan so long as his King remains in the center to obstruct the communications between his forces. Moreover, Black believes he can thwart any undue aggression.

8 N-B1 . . . .

On the way to KN3.

8 . . . . P-QN4

Not only to drive the Bishop, but also to make future prospects for the White King on the Queen-side of the board hazardous.

9 B-B2 . . . .

Temporarily the Bishop goes into hiding. It expects to emerge later on by the advance of P-Q4 or by returning to QN3. 9 B-N3 now is met by 9 . . . N-QR4; and, since the Bishop has a more promising future than the Knight, White has to retreat and lose time.

9 . . . . P-Q4

Black forces the play in the center so as to take the sting out of any contemplated adverse attack on the wing.

10 Q-K2 . . . .

White avoids the exchange of Queens, in the event Black swaps Pawns. White wishes to retain his Queen for prospective attacking chances. Incidentally, 10 PxP grants Black control of the center.

10 . . . . R-K1

Black creates a retreat for the King Bishop at KB1 and in-directly defends the King Pawn in the event White exchanges Pawns.

11 P-KR3 . . . .

White aims to prevent the pin of his King Knight and also to set up a prop for a possible future King-side Pawn advance against the Black King.

11 . . . . PxP

Black opens the Queen file and an important diagonal on which his Queen Bishop can operate. Black is contemplating the maneuver . . . B-K3-B5.

12 PxP   B-K3

In order to penetrate with *13* . . . B-B5 and drive the
White Queen to what appears to be a less favorable post.

13 N-N5! . . . .

Practical Chess Openings * gives *13* B-Q2, instead of the
text move. Black then obtains the superior game by . . . B-B5.
For the White Queen is driven to an awkward position.

The text move vacates the square KB3 for occupation by the
Queen, in the event it is attacked. At KB3, the Queen is well
posted and does not interfere with the mobility of the other
forces.

13 . . . .   B-B5

As good as any. If the Bishop retreats, *14* B-N3 is good. If
the Bishop remains, *14* NxB gives White the advantage of the
two Bishops.

14 Q-B3   P-R3
15 P-KR4! . . . .

The point of White's 13th. Black dare not capture the
Knight and open the King Rook file. Thus, if *15* . . . PxN?; *16*
PxP, N-R2; *17* Q-R5, Black is unable to prevent an incursion of
the White men.

* Fine, R., *Practical Chess Openings*, N. Y., *McKay*.

Now White's prospects are superior. He threatens *16* N-Q2, or *16* N-K3 to exchange Knight for Bishop and break up Black's Pawn formation. In addition, there is the possibility of a King-side Pawn advance which should expose the Black King as a target.

Conclusions

In this slow line of the Ruy Lopez, favored and exploited by one time world champion W. Steinitz, White invariably obtains a deferred initiative. This takes the form of an assault against the King or seizure of the center with all that it portends, or both. Moreover, since the pattern of this line is sounder than that of the main line, the risk of error is cut to a minimum.

♚ ♛ ⎍⎍⎍⎍⎍⎍⎍⎍⎍⎍⎍⎍⎍⎍⎍ ♛ ♚

Chess Movie

DEATH OF "THE BLACK DEATH"

Essaying the variation which he refined and popularized, Wilhelm Steinitz (White) subdues English grandmaster Joseph Henry Blackburne, alias "the Black Death." The overture is on a peaceful note and turns suddenly when Steinitz castles long. London, 1876, is the scene of the play. The game begins with *1* P-K4, P-K4; *2* N-KB3, N-QB3; *3* B-N5, P-QR3; *4* B-R4, N-B3; *5* P-Q3, P-Q3; *6* P-B3, B-K2 (*see diagram No. 1*).

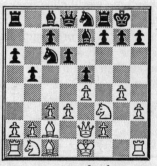

1 Now follows 7 P-KR3, O-O; 8 Q-K2, N-K1. Blackburne hopes to advance his King Bishop Pawn and gain a measure of counterplay. Steinitz checks this ambition with 9 P-KN4 and Blackburne feints on the other wing with 9 . . . P-QN4. Steinitz retreats 10 B-B2.

2 A wing development, 10 . . . B-N2 is Blackburne's choice. He hopes for the opening of the long diagonal. Steinitz plays 11 QN-Q2, heading for KB5 or ′Q5, via B1. Blackburne plays 11 . . . Q-Q2, and there follows 12 N-B1. Blackburne plays 12 . . . N-Q1, heading for KB5.

3   Both players advance their Knights on schedule: *13* N-K3, N-K3, and Steinitz enters the strategic square, *14* N-B5. There follows: . . . P-N3; *15* Nx B*ch*. To all appearances, White has wasted five moves to swap a Bishop. But he has provoked a weakness in Black's camp.

4   Blackburne recaptures *15* . . . QxN. Steinitz now sets out to exploit the weakness: *16* B-K3, N/1-N2; *17* O-O-O. This is the signal for action. With both monarchs on opposite sides of the board, it is a question of who gets there "first with the most!" White's attack, as we shall see, is much further advanced than Black's.

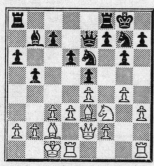

5   Blackburne plays *17* . . . P-QB4, preparing to open avenues of approach to the White King. Steinitz brazenly falls in line with *18* P-Q4. White enjoys the advantage of the Bishops. And Steinitz well knows that Bishops show up well in open positions.

6   Blackburne continues *18* . . . KPxP and Steinitz recaptures *19* PxP. Intent upon storming the White King position by a Pawn majority, Blackburne advances *19* . . . P-B5. Steinitz counters with *20* P-Q5, making room for his Bishop at Q4. Black retreats . . . N-B2.

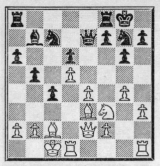

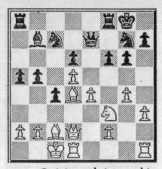

7 Steinitz plays *21* Q-Q2. When his Bishop goes to Q4, he will penetrate on the diagonal. There isn't much that Black can do to repair his own King position, so he tries to reach the White King. There follows: *21* . . . P-QR4; *22* B-Q4, P-B3. How can White open the position?

8 Steinitz brings his Queen into position: *23* Q-R6. Blackburne advances *23* . . . P-N5. Steinitz follows with *24* P-N5, clearing the diagonal of his Bishop. Blackburne parries: *24* . . . P-B4. Steinitz enters the breach with *25* B-B6. Who would think the game is nearly over?

9 Blackburne plays *25* . . . Q-B2. Now follows *26* PxP, PxP. Black's King-side barrier is being loosed from its hinges. White's Bishops are in position to administer the last rites. The Black monarch must give up the ghost beyond all peradventure of a doubt.

10 The stage is set for the finale. *27* P-N6 is the move. There follows . . . QxNP. (If *27* . . . PxP; *28* N-N5 spells *finis*.) *28* BxN and Blackburne resigns. He dare not capture the Bishop on account of R-N1, pinning the Queen, and so he cannot regain the piece lost.

7

French Defense

CLASSICAL VARIATION

THE prerogative of the first move, if properly exploited, grants White a lasting initiative. It does not, however, determine the course of the game. Black has at least an equal say in this matter.

For good and sufficient reasons, Black often directs the course of play. In doing so, he avoids lines unfamiliar to himself and arbitrarily compels his opponent to follow, rather than lead.

This does not mean that Black steals the initiative. The initiative is White's endowment. When Black originates the defense, however, he compels White to play to Black's tune. From the first move, therefore, White is burdened with the need to know all defenses which Black may use, and Black must know only one—the one which he will actually play. Ergo, to that extent, Black enjoys an edge.

Of the various defenses at Black's disposal, the prospects of the French are indeed promising; its pattern is firm, yet resilient; its snail-pace first move 1 . . . P-K3 is deceptive and often decoys an unsuspecting White into a false, impetuous attack, subject to recoil and boomerang.

The reply 1 . . . P-K3, designated at one time by the English players as "the King's Pawn One Game," was surnamed the French Defense, probably because the French writers have paid more attention to it than others. It was first mentioned, by Lucena in 1497.

It languished long, however, under what William Napier calls the "obsolete prejudice," that there was no good reason to shirk open, airy and pelting chess—and likely enough, also, under White's resentment that Black should direct the course of play. So, even after Morphy's day, his gifted and likeminded successor, Leonard, spoke of the French Defense as "the King's Pawn Sneaks One."

This defense arises as follows:

1 **P-K4   P-K3**

The advance of the King Pawn only one square, instead of two, momentarily cedes to White the greater control of the center. White's Pawn at K4 strikes the important squares, Q5

and KB5; the Black Pawn at K3 remains within Black's own half of the board. The Pawn at K3, moreover, hinders the natural mobility of Black's Queen Bishop. So, on the face of it, the defense appears foredoomed.

Such is not the case, however. These drawbacks are offset by advantages in other respects. For the Black Pawn pattern which evolves from the first move is structurally sound. White cannot pin on to a single target. Black's usual point of vulnerability, moreover, after 1 . . . P-K4, his KB2, is now safeguarded from direct attack. A White Bishop at QB4 would be biting on granite. In addition, the Pawn at K3 serves as a prop for the following move of . . . P-Q4, which is intended to challenge White's control of the center.

White's problem from the start is to capitalize on his infinitesimal center plus and free development. Black's problem is to check any undue aggression while catching up in development and locating his men in promising posts. Along these lines, the issue is drawn.

2 **P-Q4** . . . .

In nearly all cases in King Pawn openings, when an early P-Q4 can be played without incurring disadvantages, it is the proper move. As the Pawn pattern determines the character of the opening, correct strategy calls for the men to rally round the Pawns and not for the Pawns to cover haphazard development. That is why the King and Queen Pawns should take their places early, when possible.

(It should be noted that the move P-Q4 is not readily enforceable in King Pawn openings without disadvantage. For instance, after 1 P-K4, P-K4; 2 P-Q4, Black can play 2 . . . PxP and, after 3 QxP, N-QB3 gains Black a valuable tempo. In the French, the move has no drawbacks.)

2 . . . . **P-Q4**

In all King Pawn openings, the move P-Q4 for Black, is proper when it does not incur disadvantages.

3 **N-QB3** . . . .

The idea of the text move is to develop a piece and maintain pressure in the center. Various alternatives are:

(1) 3 PxP, PxP—the Exchange Variation. This line relieves the pressure in the center and leaves the Pawn structures so evenly matched that the remainder of the game is reduced to a tug of war. White still retains the minimal initiative of the first move. But, in practical play this is not sufficient to mean much.

It is important for Black to bear in mind, when playing the Exchange Variation, to avoid symmetry. Symmetrical positions are tricky. They have the earmarks of a dead draw and yet often lead to losing games for the defender. This is because the defender is unable to emulate the aggressor at some point, without risking immediate loss. A line offering good prospects for Black in the Exchange Variation runs as follows: 1 P-K4, P-K3; 2 P-Q4, P-Q4; 3 PxP, PxP; 4 N-KB3, B-Q3; 5 B-Q3, N-QB3; 6 P-B3, KN-K2; 7 O-O, B-KN5; 8 R-K1, Q-Q2; 9 QN-Q2, O-O-O; 10 P-N4, N-N3; 11 N-N3, QR-K1, with chances about even. (Maroczy vs. Spielmann, Bad Sliac, 1932.)

(2) 3 P-K5—a natural looking move, favored by Nimzóvich. Fundamentally, it is intended to usurp the terrain in the center, with White's Pawn at K5 serving as a bridgehead. Its advantages, however, are counterbalanced by disadvantages. To begin with, the time lost in moving the Pawn to K5 can be utilized to develop a piece. This, of course, is only of minor significance. More important is the fact that the bridgehead (the Pawn on K5) and its supporting props are subject to attack directly and from the wings, which will leave it in a precarious state.

On the other hand, if the Pawn at K5 can be successfully maintained, Black's position will be cramped and White may retain excellent attacking chances. The issue is drawn along these lines.

An example of this line runs as follows: 1 P-K4, P-K3; 2 P-Q4, P-Q4; 3 P-K5, P-QB4; 4 P-QB3, N-QB3; 5 N-KB3, Q-N3 (observe Black's pressure on White's Q4, which supports the bridgehead); 6 B-K2, PxP; 7 PxP, KN-K2; 8 P-QN3, N-B4; 9

B-N2, B-N5*ch*; *10* K-B1, P-KR4; *11* P-KR4, B-Q2; *12* N-B3, BxN; *13* BxB, R-QB1, with a better game for Black. In this instance, the bridgehead is still there. But White's King has been forced to move and White's general development is inferior to Black's.

The Nimzóvich Attack can also be played as a gambit, thus: *1* P-K4, P-K3; *2* P-Q4, P-Q4; *3* P-K5, P-QB4; *4* N-KB3, N-QB3; *5* B-Q3, PxP. In this line, White's plan is to maintain the Pawn at K5 at all costs, exploit the advantage of terrain to the full and attempt to recover the Pawn with the better position, as a last resort. With correct play, however, Black has little difficulty in maintaining equality.

(3) *3* N-Q2 – Tarrasch's favorite. This line will be discussed in Chapter 9.

3 . . . . N-KB3

This provocative move assists Black's development and puts pressure on White's King Pawn. 3 . . . B-N5, favored by Botvinnik, will be discussed in Chapter 8.

4 B-N5 . . . .

White pins the Knight and threatens 5 BxN to disrupt Black's Pawn formation. For Black must guard his Queen Pawn with his Queen.

Here again, *4* P-K5 has been played with moderate success. Yet, after *4* P-K5, KN-Q2, White's pressure in the center is gone and Black undermines White's King Pawn with a ceaseless bombardment of White's Q4 via . . . P-QB4, . . . N-QB3 and . . . Q-N3. To boot, a direct clash with a properly timed . . . P-KB3 will wipe out White's entire center.

4 . . . .   **B-K2**

Black breaks the pin and once again threatens White's King Pawn.

A more adventurous line for Black is *4* . . . B-N5, known as the McCutcheon Variation. Oddly enough, this line is dangerous for both sides, and its intricacies require special study.

5 **P-K5**   . . . .

There is no good way for White to maintain tension in the center any longer. That is why he now advances his King Pawn. For instance, if *5* B-Q3, PxP; *6* NxP, NxN; *7* BxB, QxB; *8* BxN, Q-N5*ch,* followed by *9* . . . QxNP, Black gains a Pawn.

The end of the tension is the signal for White to exploit to the full his gain of terrain and whatever other minor pluses he can accumulate. For now Black intends to hammer away at White's Pawn chain, and White must engage in other compensating actions.

5 . . . .   **KN-Q2**

While, in effect, the text move is a retreat, it is by no means without prospects. At Q2, the Knight bears on White's King Pawn. While the Pawn is adequately protected, its support may be unhinged as the game progresses. When, as and if the support is unhinged, the Knight at Q2 will be exerting pressure on White's King Pawn.

The more aggressive 5 . . . N-K5 is met by 6 NxN. If then 6 . . . BxB; 7 NxB, QxN; 8 P-KN3, followed by P-KB4, White's position is superior. Or if 6 NxN, PxN; 7 BxB, QxB; 8 Q-K2, Black's Pawns are structurally weaker.

6 BxB   QxB

This exchange of Bishops weakens the black squares. Naturally, when Bishops which control black squares are removed from the board, the reinforcement of the squares by the absent Bishops is impossible.

Since, however, a White and Black Bishop are swapped, who stands to gain? In this instance, White stands to gain. During the future course of the game, Black's normal play calls for the demolishing of White's Pawn center. To accomplish this, Black must play . . . P-QB4. Just as soon as this move is made, there is a vulnerable square at Black's Q3 to which a White Knight may penetrate. Moreover, when White's Queen Pawn is exchanged, White can place a Knight at Q4—a black square—and dominate a good portion of the board.

Following this thought one step further, why should Black

play . . . P-QB4 when it involves him in disadvantages? The answer is that unless Black does so, he will be more or less compelled to mark time. Then White will continue with a King-side onslaught, which is apt to be successful. Strict passivity is likely to land Black in an unbearable squeeze, with no hope of counter play.

7 P-B4 . . . .

To bolster the center and begin an attack, after the pieces are brought out, with P-KN4 and P-KB5 and a breakthrough to the Black Monarch.

7 . . . . **O-O**

This is the most active continuation for Black. It is a prelude to a head-on clash of the center Pawns which will follow in due course.

The slower positional line is 7 . . . P-QR3, intending . . . P-QB4. Observe that 7 . . . P-QB4 will not do at once because of the reply, 8 N-N5, threatening 9 N-B7*ch* to win the exchange, and also 9 N-Q6*ch*, discombobulating the Black King position. Black squares!

The positional line also results in White's favor. E.g., 7 . . . P-QR3; 8 N-B3, P-QB4; 9 PxP, N-QB3; 10 N-K2! (heading for Q4—black square!), QxP; 11 Q-Q2, P-QN4; 12 QN-Q4, NxN; 13 NxN, N-N3; 14 P-QN3, B-Q2; 15 Q-K3! R-QB1; 16 B-Q3, with a plus for White. White's centralized Knight (on a black square) and the prospects of a successful Pawn storm of the King-side rule in his favor. Black's counterplay is limited. For should he attempt . . . P-B3, to break White's center, Black will be left with a weak King Pawn which will bear constant watching.

8 Q-Q2 . . . .

The purpose of this move is to clear the last rank so that White may castle on the Queen-side. With Kings on opposite sides of the board, White is in position to start an all-out attack against the Black Monarch on the other wing.

As a general rule, a King on the Queen-side is an easier target than one on the King-side. But experience shows this position to be the exception. Most likely because White controls the center and his men are better deployed.

8 . . . . P-QB4

A good and necessary "break," with the intention of undermining White's strong hold on the center. Any delaying tactics would be met by simple development, such as N-B3, followed by B-Q3 and P-KN4, with a powerful attack in the offing.

9 N-B3   N-QB3

Putting more pressure on White's center.

10 O-O-O! . . . .

As per plan. Soon it may be a question of who gets to the adversary's King "fustest with the mostest."

10 . . . .   P-B3

To demolish White's center Pawn phalanx in order to free the Black forces for a measure of counterplay. Another way is 10 . . . P-B5, followed by . . . R-QN1 and . . . P-QN4, and a Pawn-storming of the White King position. White can meet this with a demonstration of his own, beginning with P-B5 and followed up with P-KN4. Since White is in control of the center and since his men are better poised for attack, White's chances of success should be greater.

11 PxKBP . . . .

Otherwise, Black intends . . . PxQP, followed by . . . PxKP, after which White will wind up with an isolated King Pawn. After the text move, the opening of the King file leaves Black's King Pawn a permanent target.

11 . . . . QxP

Black threatens White's King Bishop Pawn.

12 P-KN3 . . . .

Defending the Bishop Pawn and, at the same time, opening new avenues for White's Bishop at KN2 and KR3.

12 . . . . PxP

In line with the plan to dissolve the opposing center.

13 KNxP N-B4

Black's position is now free. He suffers, however, from a chronically weak, backward King Pawn.

14 B-N2 . . . .

This move makes it difficult for Black to enforce . . . P-K4. It is interesting to note that *14* B-R3 equalizes the game, thus: 14 . . . NxN; *15* QxN, QxQ; *16* RxQ, P-K4; *17* RxP, BxB; *18* RxN, PxP, with an even game in sight.

14 . . . .   **B-Q2**

Black clears his first rank so that his Rook can cooperate.

15 **KR-K1** . . . .

Pressure on the weak point.

15 . . . .   **QR-B1**

The King Pawn requires no additional defense at present. Black tries therefore, to maintain the balance of position by preparing an attack against the White King.

16 **NxN**   **RxN**

White has the better game, although adroit skill is required to prove a clear-cut advantage. A game, Stahlberg vs. Keres (Kemeri, 1937), continued from this point:

17 BxP, PxB; *18* NxP, Q-R3 (. . . Q-B2 loses to *19* R-K7, Q-B4; *20* R-K5, followed by N-K7*ch*, NxR and RxN); *19* N-K7*ch*, K-R1; *20* NxR, BxN; *21* Q-R5! White picks off another Pawn and the material remains with White having a Rook and three Pawns for two minor pieces. White won the game in 81 moves.

Conclusions

In the Classical Variation of the French Defense, White's immediate gain of the center gives him an edge which is difficult to blunt. With correct play, White should always come out on top, although the onus of finding the correct moves at each turn often proves too great in practical play.

The game in the following CHESS MOVIE illustrates the solidity of White's game in the *Classical Variation* against the French Defense.

Chess Movie

KING PAWN ONE:
KING PAWN NONE!

Tactical thrills excite even the mighty into rash action. The "irresistible" Knight "sac" at Black's 16th in the following game is only a dud. The indomitable skill of the great Akiba Rubinstein shows it up for what it is worth. Levenfish is the victim. The game was played at Carlsbad, 1911. It opens with *1* P-K4, P-K3; *2* P-Q4, P-Q4; *3* N-QB3, N-KB3; *4* B-N5, B-K2; *5* P-K5, KN-Q2; *6* BxB, QxB, reaching diagram *No. 1.*

1 The game continues: *7* Q-Q2, O-O; *8* P-B4, P-QB4; *9* N-B3, P-B3. Each side conscientiously follows the prefabricated plan with confidence in his own pattern and a crocodile's concern for the opponent's. Only the grueling test of skill and skull in the arena will be the final judgment.

2 The center dissolves with *10* PxKBP, QxP. Then White defends his KBP with *11* P-KN3. Black develops his Knight, *11 . . .* N-QB3 and *12* O-O-O, P-QR3 follows. Black is preparing a Queen-side Pawn advance. Now comes *13* B-N2, N-N3. Black has more center Pawns. Are they strong or weak?

3   It appears that Black's wing demonstration is picking up momentum. This is deceptive. For White's grip on the center checks any undue advance. There follows *14 KR-K1, N-B5; 15 Q-B2, P-QN4.* What does it matter that Black remains with a weak King Pawn—if he checkmates the White King?

4   White cuts through the Pawn avalanche with *16 PxP.* Now Black follows with his "grand combination." *16 . . . NxP* is the move. White plays *17 KxN,* and there follows *17 . . . P-N5,* recovering the piece. Momentarily, it appears that Black is scoring. White's King position is now perforated.

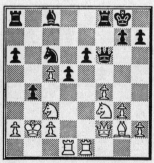

5   The atmosphere clears, however, after *18 N-Q4, PxNch; 19 K-R1.* Black's attack is running out of gas. Moreover, White's extra Bishop Pawn is no idle curiosity. It is a potential threat. And, in the background, Black's chronically weak King Pawn is the strategic target. It will figure in the denouement.

6   Black swaps Knights: *19 . . . NxN.* (What else? The threat was *20 NxP, BxN; 21 RxB, QxR; 22 BxP,* pinning the Queen.) There follows *20 QxN, R-N1; 21 R-K3, P-N4.* Black's Queen Bishop Pawn is doomed, and so Black breaks out in a new spot, to complicate and give White a chance to go wrong.

7 White continues simply with 22 RxBP. There follows 22 . . . PxP; 23 PxP, B-Q2. (White's KBP is poison. For, after 23 . . . QxP; 24 R-N3*ch* is decisive.) Even the semblance of Black's attack has vanished. . . . Now is the time to take stock. White's passed QBP looms large in the reckoning. Now what?

8 The extra Pawn advances: 24 P-B6. Black swaps Queens: 24 . . . QxQ; 25 RxQ and retreats his Bishop 25 . . . B-K1. Can the isolated Bishop Pawn be held? And at what expense? Black's survival depends on the answer to this question. Or is it too late to ask questions? The overt act is done.

9 The answer is sad! First White molests the weak King Pawn. Observe that weakness will out! 26 B-R3 is the move. Black defends with 26 . . . R-B3, and there follows 27 P-B7, R-QB1. Black's defense is hanging by a thread. How much longer can he stand the strain of White's incursion?

10 The penetrating blow is at hand. 28 RxP is *finis*. In a gesture of despair and hope, Black plays 28 . . . RxQBP. (He hopes for 29 RxR, PxR, after which he has a fighting chance.) But White continues 29 BxP*ch*. Black resigns. Curiously, the weak King Pawn falls at the very end. Poetic justice!

8

French Defense

WINAWER VARIATION

CURRENTLY in vogue is the variation of the French Defense known as the Winawer. It is an early foray of Black's King Bishop to the Queen-side of the board 3 . . . B-N5. Its popularity stems mainly from its use by world champion Botvinnik, whose constant and successful trials of it have attracted innumerable devotees.

By its very nature, the move is suspect. For Black assumes an aggressive post for his Bishop on the third move. Early aggression is part and parcel of White's stock in trade. For Black, it is almost always a violation of the precepts of good strategy.

This defense arises as follows:

1	P-K4	P-K3
2	P-Q4	P-Q4
3	N-QB3	B-N5

The Winawer Variation. By pinning the Knight, Black exerts pressure on the center and attempts to maintain equilibrium. Incidentally, Black threatens to capture White's King Pawn.

The one theoretical drawback of the move is that it practically commits Black to the eventual exchange of Bishop for Knight. Since a Bishop is minutely better than a Knight, this may wind up in White's favor.

4 P-K5   . . . .

The sharpest continuation. White establishes a salient in Black's territory, risking its collapse by counter-blows. Center tension is relaxed and, in turn, White emphasizes his gain in terrain. Note, for instance, the great sweep of both of White's Bishops and of White's Queen—how easily they can operate on the King-side of the board.

On the other hand, White's Pawn structure is now more vulnerable than Black's. Black enjoys a natural break with . . . P-QB4.

The issue is drawn along these lines.

Alternatives with the idea of maintaining the center tension are tricky. They run as follows:

(*1*) *4* N-K2. This involves the sacrifice of a Pawn. *4* . . . PxP; *5* P-QR3, B-K2; *6* NxP, N-QB3; *7* B-K3, N-B3; *8* KN-B3, O-O; *9* N-N3, P-QN3; *10* B-K2, B-N2; *11* O-O, Q-Q2; *12* Q-Q2, QR-Q1; *13* KR-Q1, Q-B1. White still retains a slight lead. This is from the fifth game of the match, Alekhine—Euwe, 1935.

(*1a*) *5* . . . BxNch; *6* NxB, P-KB4; *7* B-KB4, N-KB3; *8* Q-Q2, O-O; *9* O-O-O, N-R4; *10* B-B4, N-QB3; *11* P-B3, PxP; *12* PxP, NxB; *13* QxN. White's superior development and prospects of attack on the open King Knight file outweigh the Pawn minus.

(*2*) *4* P-QR3, BxNch; *5* PxB, PxP; *6* Q-N4, N-KB3; *7* QxNP, R-N1; *8* Q-R6, P-B4. Chances and counter-chances are rife. The position is wide open, and White still has the lead.

White can also play *4* PxP and convert the opening into one similar to the Exchange Variation of the French. Because of the balanced Pawn position, however, the prospects of injecting vitality are slim, and this method can not be termed an attempt at refutation.

4 . . . . **P-QB4**

The usual and essential counter-threat. Failure to attack White's center, either now or later, results in a one-sided game, with all the play on White's side. Pointless moves by Black will permit White to build up with, say, B-Q3, P-KB4, N-KB3, P-KN4 and P-KB5, resulting in a powerful attack. Hence, Black must engage White in the center action to forestall any such contingency.

The counter-thrust, however, may be deferred. Instead of the text move, Black may continue with *4* . . . N-K2, first. The point is that White is threatening Q-N4, aiming at Black's King Knight Pawn. It isn't easy for Black to defend the Pawn, without incurring a weakness or resorting to a counter-combination.

Consequently, *4 . . .* N-K2 anticipates Q-N4. For Q-N4 would be meaningless, if Black could reply to it simply by castling. Q-N4 may be good if, in order to defend the King Knight Pawn, Black must move his King and so forfeit the privilege of castling, or if he must advance the King Knight Pawn and so perforate his King-side Pawn position.

But *4 . . .* N-K2 does not engage White in the center soon enough and consequently has other disadvantages. Against *4 . . .* N-K2, the game might continue: *5* P-QR3, B-R4; *6* P-QN4, B-N3; *7* N-R4, B-Q2; *8* P-QB3, with a better game for White.

5 P-QR3 . . . .

It is important to "put the question" to the Bishop at the earliest convenient opportunity.

5 . . . . PxP

5 . . . BxN*ch* is also tenable, although, after *6* PxB, White's strong center and two Bishops should leave him with the advantage.

6 PxB PxN

7 Q-N4! . . . .

In effect, White is now playing a gambit, with a Pawn minus. Evidently, however, his prospects are superior. For White manages to win most of the games where Black tries to pin on to the Pawn, with 7 . . . PxP.

On the other hand, 7 PxP is the game Em. Lasker—Maroczy, New York, 1924, which favored Black (and which White won!). This game continued: 7 . . . Q-B2; 8 N-B3, N-K2; 9 B-Q3, N-N3; 10 O-O, N-Q2; 11 R-K1, QxBP.

7 . . . . P-KN3

7 . . . K-B1, forfeiting the privilege of castling, is hardly better. The text move leaves holes in Black's King-side Pawn structure.

8 N-B3 . . . .

Protecting the King Pawn and now threatening to recapture the Pawn minus.

8 . . . . Q-B2

White's superior development, plus his two Bishops, makes it imperative for Black to eye material advantages, even though he can hardly afford the time to acquire more material. A sorry state!

9 B-Q3 . . . .

Protecting the Queen Bishop Pawn, so that, if Black captures . . . PxP, the Queen Bishop Pawn will be defended. Moreover, the Bishop is pointing in the direction of Black's King-side for future reference.

9 . . . . N-QB3

Black must continue his development. If he stops for, say, 9 . . . PxP, then 10 BxP leaves Black's development lagging to a point where he will be unable to prevent some serious penetrations. White can open the position wide with P-QB4. Then the absence of Black's Bishop controlling the black squares will stick out like a sore thumb. Observe, particularly, that White can continue with P-N5, followed by B-R3, after which the Bishop enjoys a terrific sweep of the diagonal.

10 O-O . . . .

White can defend the King Pawn, if he so desires, by *10 Q-KB4*. He prefers not to, for he rightly feels that Black will not have the time to go Pawn-grabbing. Therefore, he continues his development.

10 . . . . KN-K2

You might inquire, however, why not *10 . . . NxKP?* Black might as well be hanged for a sheep as for a lamb. If *10 . . . NxKP; 11 NxN, QxN; 12 B-KB4*, observe that both of White's Bishops are operating, that White's Queen is well posted, that White is castled and that Black hasn't a single piece out, other than his Queen. Given such a position, you know that White must have something, that it is up to you to find it. You will not necessarily be able to win on the following move, but you can continue to make it uncomfortable for Black to the point where he will be unable to put up resistance. One thing, however, you must bear in mind. The basis of your advantage is the possibility of an attack. Hence, you must not swap Queens, unless, of course, you can win a piece in doing so. For your Queen is the most important piece in any brewing attack. Experiment with this position for some time and you will convince yourself how easy it is to bring matters to a head.

11 R-K1   . . . .

White defends the King Pawn. By the same reasoning as before, you might inquire, why defend the King Pawn, why not let it go? To begin with, your Rook defends the King Pawn not only for the sake of the Pawn but also because it operates well on the open King file. Moreover, as Black catches up in his development, the sacrifice of additional material is apt to be unsound.

11 . . . .   B-Q2

Black is still intent on catching up his laggard development. Yes, he can toy with the tainted 11 . . . PxP; but after 12 QBxP, his defensive chores are more difficult and his means possibly inadequate under any circumstances.

12 PxP   . . . .

Now White retrieves his Pawn in order to free his Queen Bishop for action.

White is for choice.

There is no safety for the Black Monarch on either wing. For instance, if 12 . . . O-O, White infiltrates with 13 Q-N5, followed by 14 Q-R6, 15 N-N5 or 15 B-N5-B6. Black has no adequate defense.

A game Bogolyubov–Danielsson, Zoppot, 1935, continued as follows: 12 . . . O-O-O; 13 P-N5, N-QN1; 14 Q-N4, B-K1;

15 B-N5, R-Q2; *16* RxP, Q-N3; *17* R-R8, Q-Q1; *18* N-Q4, P-R3;
19 B-B6, R-N1; *20* P-N6, *Resigns*.

Conclusions

The Winawer Variation of the French Defense has enjoyed
a measure of success in tournament practice. This is based not
so much on its theoretical accuracy, but rather on its practical
exponent, Mikhail Botvinnik, chess champion of the world.

This much can be said in its favor. The patterns which
evolve are different and call for sharp play on White's part.

Chess Movie

THE SQUIRM WILL TURN

S TOUT heart does not a chessplayer make. But it saves many a game! Many a Black would throw in the towel with Ragozin's position at move 22. But not Ragozin! Out of nothing, he fabricates a mating net, and poor Lilienthal is enmeshed. The game was played in Moscow in 1944. It opens with: *1* P-K4, P-K3; *2* P-Q4, P-Q4; *3* N-QB3, B-N5; *4* P-K5, P-QB4 (*see diagram No. 1*).

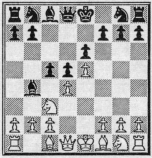 

1 There follows 5 P-QR3, BxN*ch;* 6 PxB, N-K2; 7 N-B3, B-Q2. Lilienthal will try to capitalize his stronger center, his two Bishops and the greater terrain. Ragozin will pin on to the superior Pawn position. Each player will have his day in court, and judgment will be rendered under due process.

2 Lilienthal plays 8 P-QR4. He hopes to decoy Black forces to the mangy Pawn. The game continues . . . Q-R4; 9 B-Q2, P-B5. The board has been rent in two. The King-side belongs to White; the Queen-side is Black's. And Black is ready to collect Pawnence! The isolated Pawn is doomed.

3 White prepares the entry of his King Bishop with *10* P-N3, and Black fortifies himself with . . . B-B3. Then follows *11* B-R3, N-Q2; *12* O-O, N-QN3. Black is making assurance triply sure; the Queen Rook Pawn will not escape. That, however, is old stuff. What goes on the other side?

4 White continues with *13* N-R4, and Black plays . . . NxP. Now White plays *14* P-B4, planning a break-through on that wing, which Black checks with . . . P-KN3. Or does he? White follows through with *15* P-B5. He must make progress at all cost. Yet can this sacrifice be progress?

5 Black captures *15* . . . KPxP, and now comes the point. White plays *16* P-N4! There is no way for Black to prevent the opening of a file and a diagonal. Black hies himself to the other side of the board with *16* . . . O-O, and there follows *17* PxP, PxP. One Pawn is coming home. Then what?

6 There follows *18* NxP, NxN; *19* BxN*ch*, K-N1; *20* B-R3, QR-KB1. The atmosphere has cleared somewhat. Black is a Pawn plus. Black's King Bishop Pawn, however, is an easy target, and White has all the play. If Black's King Bishop Pawn falls, White's King Pawn will assume a stellar role.

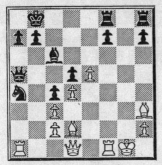

7 White plays 21 K-R1 to get out of any counter checks. Black plays . . . KR-N1. Then follows 22 Q-R5, Q-B2; 23 R-B6?? (after 23 B-B4, Black could hardly survive). To all intents and appearances, White is progressing rapidly. Is he not hammering away at Black's weaknesses?

8 Now comes a surreptitious surprise. Black replies 23 . . . N-B4! White captures 24 PxN, and then continues . . . P-Q5ch. White interposes 25 R-B3, and there follows: 25 . . . P-B3; 26 P-K6. Even now, White appears reasonably happy. But he reckons without his host. He is soon rudely awakened.

9 26 . . . Q-K4 is the sockdolager. White cannot afford to swap Queens, nor can he afford not to! He plays 27 B-N4, and the game continues . . . P-B4; 28 B-R3, Q-K7. How the picture has changed in a few short moves. A moment ago, Black was on the run. Now White barely manages to keep going.

10 White continues with 29 B-B4ch, and Black replies . . . K-R1. Then White plays 30 R-KB1. Again, it seems that White is coming out on top. But Black puts an end to all conjecture with 30 . . . R-N5, cutting the communication between the Queen and Rook. Nought is to be done. White resigns.

9

French Defense

TARRASCH VARIATION

THERE is another way of treating the French Defense. It is to play N-Q2 on White's third move. This method may well be labeled Tarrasch's line, after its leading exponent of several decades ago. Even today, however, the line is in vogue.

While the Classical and Winawer Variations lead to academic pluses for White, they are beset with practical problems. In the Classical, for instance, White is compelled to lock the center comparatively early and absorb pummeling blows in his own mid-section. In the Winawer, White must submit to an annoying, even though innocuous pin. By maintaining a fluid center and avoiding the pin, the Tarrasch aims to retain the good features of the other variations and discard the bad ones.

This line arises as follows:

1 P-K4   P-K3

2 P-Q4   P-Q4

3 N-Q2 . . . .

The Tarrasch. White protects his King Pawn via N-Q2, instead of N-QB3, averts the annoying pin *3* . . . B-N5 and keeps open the fortifying move of P-QB3, in the event it is necessary.

Its main drawback is that the Knight at Q2 fails to exert pressure on Black's Queen Pawn, which, in turn, gives Black more leeway than in the other variations. The temporary blockade of White's Queen Bishop is of minor significance. In many variations the Queen Bishop does not take an active part in the early play; in others, the Knight clears the path when necessary.

3 . . . . **P-QB4**

Because White's Queen Knight is not bearing down on Black's Queen Pawn and because White's Queen is also obstructed in its view of the Queen file, Black can afford to intensify the center tension with the text move. If White's Queen Knight were at B3, Black's Queen Pawn would become a comparatively easy target.

Another way for Black is *3* . . . N-KB3, as in the Classical. This line might pursue the following course, taken from

a game Alekhine–Capablanca, AVRO, 1938: *4* P-K5, KN-Q2;
5 B-Q3, P-QB4; *6* P-QB3, N-QB3; *7* N-K2, Q-N3; *8* N-B3, PxP;
9 PxP, B-N5*ch;* *10* K-B1, B-K2; *11* P-QR3, N-B1; *12* P-QN4, B-
Q2; *13* B-K3, N-Q1; *14* N-B3, P-QR4; *15* N-R4, Q-R2; *16* P-N5,
P-N3; *17* P-N3, P-B4; *18* K-N2, with a far superior game for
White. Observe the cluster of Black men in the center and the
disunity of Black's forces.

Note also that White locks the center with *4* P-K5, as in
the Classical. The main difference, however, between this
line and the Classical is that White has the move P-QB3 in
reserve to fortify his center. Consequently, White is able to
maintain the center with Pawns and utilize his pieces for
advantage in other directions.

A somewhat irregular try for Black is *3* . . . N-QB3. Then
might follow *4* KN-B3, N-B3; *5* P-K5, N-Q2, with advantage
for White. Here again, White takes the rigid center, since
Black is unable to crack down upon it with the usual . . . P-
QB4, at least until he makes adequate preparations.

4 KPxP . . . .

The point of this move is to leave Black a comparative
choice of evils. *4* KN-B3 is also good, but more complicated.

4 . . . .   KPxP

This results in an isolated Pawn for Black. After *4* . . .
QxP, however, White continues in gambit fashion with KN-B3

and gains the lead in development. If then, for example, 5 . . .
PxP; 6 B-B4, followed by 7 O-O; 8 Q-K2; 9 N-N3; and, if
necessary, 10 R-Q1 and the recovery of the Pawn with a
powerful position. Should Black attempt to hold the Pawn
with . . . P-K4, he will fail. For his King Pawn as well as
his King will become exposed.

Black, of course, need not accept the gambit Pawn. The
game might be played as follows: 4 . . . QxP; 5 KN-B3, N-
QB3; 6 B-B4, Q-Q1; 7 N-N3. But it is clear that White gains
a substantial lead in development.

5 B-N5*ch* . . . .

Usually a check of this nature is to be discounted. For
White's Bishop is better deployed in some attack, rather than
a positional pin.

Here there is a point to the check. Since Black is going
to be left with an isolated Queen Pawn, White has already
established his advantage. Now he does not mind swapping:
the more he swaps, the less opportunity will there be for Black
of gaining compensation for the defect in his Pawn structure.

White has no intention, of course, of an immediate swap
which reinforces the isolani. Nor does he intend to trade
Bishop for Knight, without some gain in return.

5 . . . .   N-B3
6 Q-K2*ch* . . . .

Pursuing the plan of leading to an endgame in which Black suffers from an isolated Queen Pawn.

6 .... **Q-K2**

Practically forced. If *6 . . .* B-K2; 7 PxP and White can maintain the Pawn plus. If *6 . . .* B-K3; 7 KN-B3, and White threatens *8* PxP, followed by *9* N-N3 and *10* QN-Q4, with terrific pressure against Black's Queen Knight and Queen Bishop. Black will experience difficulty warding this off.

7 **PxP   QxQ**ch

Otherwise, White will defend and retain the extra Pawn.

8 **NxQ   BxP**

Now White enjoys a handsome lead in development. This, plus Black's isolated Pawn rules in White's favor. The only thing that might be said for Black is that he experiences more freedom than is usual for Black.

9 N-QN3   B-N3

10 QN-Q4 . . . .

A game Euwe—Botvinnik, World's Championship, The Hague, 1948, continued with *10* B-Q2 and resulted in a draw, after particularly alert defense on the part of Botvinnik.

The text move is consonant with the theme of White's opening play, which is pressure, direct or otherwise, against Black's Queen Pawn. Euwe's *10* B-Q2 appears to be too labored.

White is for choice. He might continue with *11* B-KB4, followed by *12* O-O-O, and then pile up on Black's Queen Pawn. This he can do by doubling Rooks on the Queen file and/or swinging his King Bishop to QN3.

Conclusions

In the main variation, the Black side of the Tarrasch leaves much to be desired by Black. Saddled with an isolated Pawn in what is virtually an endgame, the prospects are decidedly uninviting even though Black may be able to eke out a draw.

Unless some way can be found to bolster Black's play in the main or subsidiary lines, the Tarrasch will compel masters to shy away from the French. The spectacle of the isolani, however, should not instill fear in others than masters.

Chess Movie

CAPA COMES A CROPPER

Weakness will out. It will assert itself in the remotest corners of the board, far removed from the intrinsic defect. Thus Capablanca's weak Queen Bishop Pawn makes him fall prey to Keres' King-side assault on the other wing at the fabulous AVRO Tournament of 1938. The game begins with: *1* P-K4, P-K3; *2* P-Q4, P-Q4; *3* N-Q2, P-QB4; *4* KPxP, KPxP (*see diagram No. 1*).

1 There follows 5 KN-B3, N-QB3; *6* B-N5, Q-K2*ch*. Capablanca (Black) wishes to swap Queens. Even he has a healthy respect for Keres' flamboyant nature. But the wily Keres will not swap. 7 B-K2 is the move. True, the Queen Pawn is inadequately defended. That doesn't matter. Capa plays 7 . . . PxP.

2 Keres plays 8 O-O, and Capa replies . . . Q-B2. He will not leave his Queen in the crossfire of a White Rook at King square. The game continues 9 N-N3, B-Q3; *10* QNxP, and White has retrieved his Pawn. The threat is now N-N5. Capa parries: *10* . . . P-QR3. Then comes *11* P-QN3, KN-K2.

3 Keres now usurps the long diagonal with 12 B-N2, and the game continues . . . O-O; 13 NxN. Keres consolidates Black's Pawns, only to create a target in the new cluster. There follows . . . PxN; 14 P-B4, B-K3; 15 Q-B2, PxP; 16 BxBP, BxB; 17 QxB. The QP has become an isolated BP.

4 Capa seeks scope for his men and plays 17 . . . KR-N1. There follows 18 P-KR3, R-N4; 19 QR-B1, R-QB1. Capa believes in over-protection of weak spots. Now comes 20 KR-Q1, N-N3; 21 N-Q4. The target is under fire and requires additional support. A good Pawn is at stake.

5 Capa defends with 21 . . . R-N3, and then comes a bombastic surprise with 22 N-K6. The Knight is immune, and it is headed for the Black King. Capa replies . . . Q-N1, and there follows 23 N-N5, R-N2; 24 Q-KN4. The scene of combat has changed. Keres is focusing his attention on the King.

6 Capa continues 24 . . . B-B5, and Keres replies 25 R-B4. Capa's Rook again pops up with . . . R-N4. In the background is the isolated Pawn, for future reference if need be. At hand is a concealed sockdolager, 26 NxBP! Now the barrier to the monarch is broken down. Soon the men will penetrate.

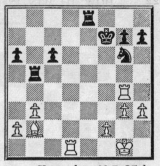

7 Capa plays 26 . . . R-K1, and Keres follows with 27 P-N3. Capa continues . . . Q-B1, and a general exchange ensues: 28 RxB, QxQ; 29 RxQ, KxN. Oddly enough, the isolated Pawn is to blame for Black's loss on the other wing. And it still remains to be attacked. But first, Keres can pick up another Pawn.

8 Keres plays 30 R-Q7ch, and Capa interposes . . . R-K2. Keres swaps Rooks: 31 RxRch, KxR, and then he swipes the second Pawn: 32 BxP. The rest is the law of inertia. Capa in motion cannot stop; otherwise he might resign. For two Pawns minus is not a death warrant. It is death.

9 Now come the feeble gestures. Capa plays 32 . . . R-QR4, and Keres defends with 33 P-QR4. Capa replies with . . . R-QB4, and Keres with 34 R-N4. Capa continues: 34 . . . K-K3. To the bitter end, the spectators expect a miracle from the former world champion. It is not to be.

10 Keres gets down to business. The mopping-up operation was a success. Now for the finishing touches. 35 K-N2 is the move. Capa replies . . . P-KR4. There follows 36 R-QB4, RxR; 37 PxR, K-Q3; 38 P-B4, and the invincible Cuban resigns. And the isolated Pawn is still there!

10

Sicilian Defense

THE MODERN DRAGON VARIATION

The Sicilian Defense, *1* P-K4, P-QB4—a half hold on the center—is the most aggressive of all the comparatively sound defenses at Black's command. From its very beginning, an unbalanced Pawn formation arises, which gives opportunity to both contestants to explore advantages in different directions. The result is unabated action.

The favored line of the Sicilian is known as the "Dragon" Variation. Its name cannot be traced with certainty but is most likely derived from Black's Pawn pattern in the early stages of play—as seen here, it most definitely forms a serpentine outline.

The Sicilian dates from Polerio, 1590. Receiving scant attention in its incipience, its popularity rose with the celebrated MacDonnell—Labourdonnais match of 1834 and the Staunton—St. Amant match of 1843. The great London tournament of 1851 marked the occasion of its first practical test, after which it was relegated to limbo. Since then, it has been revived on and off with intermittent success, and its present rating is on the ascent.

The "Dragon" arises as follows:

1 P-K4   P-QB4

The Sicilian Defense. The move *1 . . . P-QB4* incorporates a number of ideas. To begin with, it avoids symmetry in the Pawn pattern. Thus, instead of the tedious attempt to neutralize White's initiative, it is an independent action and calls for original planning on the part of the aggressor.

Theoretically, as between White's first move and Black's, White enjoys the edge. White's Pawn at K4 strikes at Q5 and KB5—a center and a near-center square—and Black's Pawn at QB4 strikes at Q5 and QN5—a center and a non-center square. So White's move is more dominating. Yet Black's has its point. To all intents and purposes, it divides the board in two: White commands the King's wing and Black, the Queen's. As the Kings abide on the King-side, Black's plan is to check any undue aggression there and expand on the far side, where he often gains an endgame advantage. For the same reason, however, White dominates the more vital terrain.

2 N-KB3 . . . .

A good developing move with an eye to supporting the following move of P-Q4. The immediate 2 P-Q4 will not do because of . . . PxP; 3 QxP, N-QB3, gaining a valuable tempo for Black.

The ancient alternative, 2 P-QB3, with a view to establishing a Pawn center, is of doubtful merit. For, after 2 P-QB3, Black can reply . . . P-Q4 and obtain a free and easy game. As a rule, Black cannot play . . . P-Q4 in the early stages of play for then White captures PxP and, on . . . QxP, gains time by attacking the Queen with N-QB3. Once White plays P-QB3, however, and preempts the square QB3, Black can safely play . . . P-Q4. For he no longer need fear N-QB3 and the loss of the tempo.

Another way of continuing is 2 N-QB3. This, however, is not a sharp attempt to obtain minute advantages out of the opening. It is the prelude to a slow, positional, planned development which can be met by an equally good counter-development. The resulting position leads to an even game, thus: 2 N-QB3, N-QB3; 3 P-KN3, P-KN3; 4 B-N2, B-N2; 5 P-Q3, P-K3; 6 B-K3, Q-R4; 7 N-K2, N-Q5; 8 O-O, N-K2; 9 K-R1, O-O; 10 P-QR3, KN-B3; 11 R-QN1, P-Q3; 12 P-QN4, Q-Q1; 13 Q-Q2, R-N1; 14 B-N5, Q-K1.

2 . . . . P-Q3

At this point, Black has a choice of moves, among which are the usual 2 . . . N-QB3 and the less usual 2 . . . N-KB3. These moves, however, may involve Black as the butt of a particularly critical attack, for example, the Richter Attack after 2 . . . N-QB3. Hence the modern text move, which enables Black to reach a comparatively sound and promising development, without much ado.

3 P-Q4 . . . .

White's plan is to nullify any hold which Black exercises on White's Q4 and, at the same time, maintain and build up his own grip on the center. In doing this, however, he makes a somewhat uneven exchange. He swaps his Queen Pawn—a good center Pawn—for Black's Bishop Pawn—not a center Pawn. Insofar as White's hold on the center is enhanced, the move is good. Over the long term, Black's extra center Pawn should stand him in good stead. Consequently, White's plan is to capitalize his advantage—greater control of the center and terrain—in the near future. Whereas Black attempts to neutralize White's advantage and remain with the extra center Pawn. These considerations are germane to the text move.

Again, White cannot very well build up a Pawn center with 3 P-QB3, to be followed by P-Q4. For, if 3 P-QB3, N-KB3, White's unguarded King Pawn requires an awkward defense—if his Queen Pawn is slated for Q4.

3 . . . .   PxP

White threatens 4 PxP, PxP; 5 QxQ*ch*, denying Black the privilege of castling. Since there is no other good way of preventing this, Black exchanges.

Certain advantages, however, accrue to Black from the exchange. First, he swaps an inferior Pawn for a superior one. Also, he opens his Queen Bishop file for future use.

4 NxP . . . .

Not *4* QxP, as . . . N-QB3 gains a tempo.

4 . . . . N-KB3!

An important interpolation. The text move is not just a developing move. It is *the* developing move. Any other may involve Black in serious positional difficulties. It is necessary to understand the reason for this.

White's mainstay in the center is his King Pawn. If this falls or is exchanged or if Black establishes a strong Pawn of his own in the center, then White's control vanishes—while Black remains with an extra center Pawn. So Black eyes the possibility of . . . P-Q4, constantly. Technically, however, *4* . . . P-Q4 is impossible. If *4* . . . P-Q4, then 5 PxP, QxP; *6* N-QB3, and White is too far ahead in development. But Black must keep the possibility open. If he continues with any move, say *4* . . . P-KN3, White replies with 5 P-QB4 and closes the chance of . . . P-Q4 forever more. If White succeeds, moreover, in playing P-QB4, he nullifies all the pressure which Black hopes to exert on his own, open Queen Bishop file. The text move precludes the possibility of P-QB4 for White, under favorable circumstances, and keeps White constantly on guard against a Black . . . P-Q4.

5 N-QB3 . . . .

This blocks the move P-QB4. Black need no longer concern himself over that possibility.

There are, indeed, other ways for White to protect his King Pawn and still retain the option of playing P-QB4. But they leave much to be desired. For instance, if 5 P-KB3, P-K4; 6 N-N5, P-QR3; 7 N/5-B3, B-K3, and there is no good way of preventing 8 . . . P-Q4. Thus, if 8 N-Q5, NxN; 9 PxN, B-Q2, Black's Pawn pattern is better.

Note that 6 . . . P-Q4 will not do: 7 PxP, NxP; 8 QxN, QxQ; 9 N-B7*ch*, and a full piece accrues to White.

5 . . . . P-KN3

The Dragon Variation. Black intends to fianchetto his King Bishop and so dominate the long diagonal throughout the center of the board.

Observe here that Black cannot play 5 . . . P-Q4. For, after 6 PxP, NxP; 7 B-N5*ch*, Black has no good move.

6 B-K2 . . . .

A good post for the Bishop. For it clears the path for castling and prevents Black from playing . . . N-N5 later on. Of course, 6 . . . N-N5 is meaningless. But, in some contingencies, say when White develops his Queen Bishop at K3, the move may be purposeful.

6 P-KN3, followed by 7 B-N2 is also good for White, inasmuch as it practically prevents . . . P-Q4 for all time.

Another possibility is 6 P-B4 in attempt to refute Black's

formation by storm. In that case, Black must play carefully, for a misstep will be fatal. Thus, if *6* P-B4, best is *6 . . .* N-B3. Then, if *7* NxN, PxN; *8* P-K5, N-Q2, Black's position is tenable. The following gamelet is indicative of what can happen when Black goes astray; *6* P-B4, B-N2?; *7* P-K5, PxP; *8* PxP, N-Q4; *9* B-N5*ch*, K-B1; *10* O-O, BxP; *11* B-R6*ch*, K-N1; *12* NxN, QxN; *13* N-B5! Q-B4*ch*; *14* K-R1, Q-B2; *15* B-QB4, BxN; *16* RxB, B-B3, and White mates in five!—*17* Q-Q5, P-K3; *18* QxKP, PxQ; *19* BxP*ch*, Q-B2; *20* RxB and mate next move (Horowitz—Carrigan, simultaneous exhibition).

$$6 \ . \ . \ . \ . \ \ \textbf{B-N2}$$
$$7 \ \textbf{O-O} \quad \ \ \textbf{O-O}$$

Development goes on apace. Black now threatens to get the better game with *8 . . .* P-Q4.

$$8 \ \textbf{N-N3} \ . \ . \ . \ .$$

To clear the Queen file so Black is unable to play *. . .* P-Q4.

$$8 \ . \ . \ . \ . \ \ \textbf{N-B3}$$

Developing—so as not to interfere with the mobility of the other men.

$$9 \ \textbf{P-B4} \ . \ . \ . \ .$$

Preparing for a King-side Pawn assault and also making way for *10* B-B3 to prevent . . . P-Q4. In this way, White sews up control of the center.

9 . . . . P-QR3

So that Black's Queen can establish a haven at Black's QB2 without fear of being molested by a White Knight at its QN5. Also, Black is preparing a Queen-side Pawn advance for the future.

It is possible for Black to play *9* . . . P-QN4 without losing a Pawn. This, however, is a somewhat involved combination. Thus, if *9* . . . P-QN4; *10* BxP, NxP! whatever piece White captures, Black is able to recover with *11* . . . Q-N3*ch*. White, however, retains the better game simply with *10* B-B3.

10 B-B3   Q-B2

White is for choice because of his control of the center, though play is extremely difficult for both sides.

White's further plan may consist of a King-side Pawn assault, beginning with P-N4. This is perilous, however, in the event that it miscarries. White may occupy Q5 or the open Queen file or try to utilize all the different advantages in conjunction with each other.

Black has prospects on the open Queen Bishop file, after developing his Queen Bishop either at Q2 or K3. He may maneuver a Knight to QB5, where it exerts a bind on the Queen-side, and follow with a Queen-side Pawn advance.

Conclusions

The Modern Dragon Variation of the Sicilian Defense offers Black about as good prespects as Black can expect in any line. While, theoretically White is for choice, practically, the onus of proving the advantage rests on White, and a misstep can be fatal—to White.

Chess Movie

CLASH OF CHAMPIONS!

W HEN the irresistible Alekhine meets the immovable Botvinnik, what happens? Chaos? . . . No, just a rollicking jamboree, with chessmen being blown to the four winds. This game between world champion Alekhine and the future world champion Botvinnik was played at Nottingham, 1936. It opens with *1* P-K4, P-QB4; *2* N-KB3, P-Q3; *3* P-Q4, PxP; *4* NxP, N-KB3; *5* N-QB3, P-KN3; *6* B-K2, B-N2 (*see diagram No. 1*).

1 There follows 7 B-K3, N-B3; *8* N-N3. Alekhine prevents the freeing move of . . . P-Q4. Botvinnik, however, continues with *8* . . . B-K3, preparing the Pawn advance and eyeing Black's strategic QB5 for future reference. Alekhine plays *9* P-B4, and Botvinnik follows with *9* . . . O-O.

2 The usual move here is the safe and sane *10* O-O. But usual moves are foreign to world champion Alekhine. He will make the move that will hurl his opponent from the *Sessel*—something original that will teach this pretender a lesson. *10* P-N4 is the move. It signals an attack.

3 Botvinnik hurls defiance at his noted adversary. He will not be scared into abject retreat. Despite the vise-like grip which White maintains on his Q5, Botvinnik assails the mid-section. 10 . . . P-Q4 is his adventurous reply. The ensuing complications baffle even the giants of chessdom.

4 There follows 11 P-B5, B-B1; 12 KPxP, N-N5. Botvinnik has sacrificed a Pawn but now threatens to recover it. If Alekhine relinquishes his material plus, his position will remain in tatters. What devilish continuation can infuse new life into what is becoming a mere matter of technique?

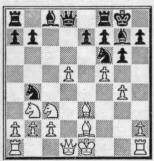

5 13 P-Q6 is the problem-like rejoinder. To 13 . . . QxP, Alekhine replies 14 B-B5, forking Queen and Knight. Again, Botvinnik has to escape from a predicament. It is important to keep track of material. For the day of reckoning may not be far off, and material still has its relative value.

6 Botvinnik defends his Knight with 14 . . . Q-B5. Alekhine chases the Queen by 15 R-KB1. A Black "critter" is doomed. Still Alekhine's King Rook Pawn is en prise, and Botvinnik stoops to pick this up with 15 . . . QxRP. No equivalent for a Knight. But open lines to the White King promise action.

7 There follows *16 BxN, NxP*. Another "critter" is immolated on Caissa's altar to pacify the White monarch. This method of making peace is no olive branch variety; it is the meat cleaver! The throne of the White King is demanded, and Black will not abide a sultry "no" by way of an answer.

8 Alekhine plays *17 BxN*, out of compulsion, and *17 . . . Q-N6ch* is the reply. Now Alekhine has two pieces for a few paltry Pawns. But what can he do? Not K-K2, Botvinnik would take a Bishop with a check and one without. Nor K-Q2 either, because of . . . B-R3*ch* with even more dire consequences.

9 Alekhine plays *18 R-B2*, Botvinnik follows with . . . Q-N8*ch*. Again, what is Alekhine to do? Not K-K2. For it still loses both his Bishops. Nor yet K-Q2. For it would cost all his material gain, and, to boot, his King would fall. Still he has a preponderance of material. He may find something.

10 The spectators wait with bated breath. Surely, the world champion will pick something out of the thin air. . . . Alekhine, however, retires gracefully with *19 R-B1*. The move signifies his intention to draw, and a draw is agreed upon by the contestants. What a pretty finish. Perpetual check!

11

Queen's Gambit Declined

Tʜᴇ unostentatious move *1* P-Q4 is nowadays considered the most effective way of beginning a game of chess. This is evinced by a preponderance of Queen Pawn games in modern master tournaments.

Odd, indeed, is the apparent reappraisal of this debut. It was first mentioned in the Göttingen Manuscript of 1490. And not until the Vienna Tournament of 1873 — nearly four hundred years later — did it receive any legitimate recognition.

There is, of course, room for argument over the relative merits of *1* P-Q4 as against other opening moves. This much, however, can be said in its favor. It leads to structurally sound patterns of play, with few intrinsic defects; it averts surprise mating attacks—for the White King is generously protected; it restricts the adversaries' defenses to the sparser branches of the Queen Pawn and, consequently, permits White to concentrate on only a few lines; and it affords excellent prospects for slow but sure progress.

Preliminary move in the Queen's Gambit Declined is usually 1 P-Q4. Often, however, the same patterns are reached by a transposition of moves.

The opening arises as follows:

1 P-Q4 . . . .

The advance of the Pawn to Q4 embodies many purposes.

(1) *Control of the center*. The Pawn at Q4 strikes at the important central square K5 and the square on the rim of the center, QB5.

(2) *Freedom of action*. The advance of the Queen Pawn releases White's Queen and Queen Bishop for future action.

(3) *Safety of the King*. When White plays 1 P-K4, Black often effectively posts a Bishop at Black's QB4, pointing at the White King's field. 1 P-Q4 averts even this latent threat.

1 . . . . P-Q4

Black follows suit for the same reasons. Alternative lines of play such as 1 . . . N-KB3 or 1 . . . P-K3 may lead to the same opening by transposition of moves. Or they may lead to independent defenses, not within the scope of the Queen's Gambit Declined.

2 P-QB4 . . . .

The Queen's Gambit. White offers a Pawn in order to decoy Black's center Pawn from its control of vital squares.

2 . . . . P-K3

The most popular defense, since it has been extensively analyzed. According to the results of the analysis, Black is able to hold his own, with precision defense.

The paramount drawback of the move is that it locks in Black's Queen Bishop. From here on, Black is saddled with the problem of developing this Bishop, which is often referred to as the "problem Bishop."

The question arises: why lock in the Bishop? Why not continue with 2 . . . P-QB3 and bring out the Bishop later on? The fact is that 2 . . . P-QB3 is quite playable. But not for the reason that Black will be able to bring out the Bishop.

Black's Queen Bishop is tied to the defense of Black's Queen Knight Pawn. As soon as the Bishop moves, White continues with Q-N3 and attacks the Knight Pawn. Black must then defend the Pawn. He can do so by playing . . . Q-B1. Then, however, his Queen is relegated to the menial task of defending a Pawn—a sorry job for the Queen. Or he can do so by advancing his Queen Knight Pawn to QN3. The advance of this Pawn leaves a marked weakness on the white squares in Black's Queen-side Pawn structure. Such a weakness can be exploited profitably by the expert. Hence Black reconciles himself to retaining the Queen Bishop on its original square until some such time in the future that he is able to bring it out, without damaging his position. And he willingly locks in the Bishop for the present by the text move as being the wisest of unhappy choices.

The alternative 2 . . . P-QB3, however, is good. In fact, it is the theoretical rejoinder. For should White capture 3 PxP,

Black can recapture with the Bishop Pawn and keep the Pawn formation in symmetrical balance. On the contrary, after 2 . . . P-K3; 3 PxP, PxP, White remains with two center Pawns —the King Pawn and the Queen Pawn—as against Black's one Pawn—the Queen Pawn.

Despite these considerations, the text move is more often employed. Black has a difficult position, in any event; and it is merely a question of which defense Black prefers to suffer through before he can reach equality.

2 . . . PxP is the Queen's Gambit Accepted, which, in a sense, is not a valid gambit insofar as White can recover the Pawn at will.

After 2 . . . PxP, the continuation runs as follows: 3 N-KB3, N-KB3; 4 P-K3, and Black makes no effort to defend his extra Bishop Pawn, which is attacked by White's King Bishop. A defense will be of no avail, thus: 4 . . . P-QN4; 5 P-QR4, P-B3; 6 PxP, PxP; 7 P-QN3; Now, if 7 . . . PxP; 8 BxPch, followed by 9 QxP, recovers the Pawn with the better position.

It is to be noted that after 1 P-Q4, P-Q4; 2 P-QB4, Black must either accept the gambit, resort to a speculative counter-gambit, or protect his Queen Pawn with a Pawn. Should Black make any old developing move at this stage, White will gain an advantage. For example, if 2 . . . N-KB3; 3 PxP. Now, if 3 . . . QxP; 4 N-QB3, and White's development has been enhanced at Black's expense. Or, if 3 . . . NxP; 4 P-K4, and White's has established a superior center at Black's expense.

3 N-QB3 . . . .

A good developing move, exerting pressure on the center.

3 PxP, known as the Exchange Variation, also offers excellent prospects. In making the exchange, White expects to profit from his extra center Pawn and the newly-opened Queen Bishop file on which he can exercise permanent pressure during the future course of the game. On the other hand, the exchange ends the tension in the center and frees Black's

problem Bishop. The sum total of pluses and minuses, in the opinion of the experts, seems to favor the text move.

3 . . . . N-KB3

A good developing move, defending the center and clearing Black's first rank in order to make early castling possible.

If 3 . . . PxP, the game reverts to the Queen's Gambit Accepted.

4 B-N5 . . . .

Putting additional pressure on the center, White threatens to continue with 5 BxN. For, if . . . QxB; 6 PxP, PxP; 7 NxP gains a Pawn. Or, if 5 . . . PxB, Black's King-side Pawn position is shattered.

4 . . . . QN-Q2!

An indirect defense of the Queen Pawn, involving a pretty trap.

Again, if 4 . . . PxP, White has no difficulty in retrieving the Pawn by 5 P-K3.

5 P-K3 . . . .

White now defends the gambit Pawn, so that he need no longer concern himself with whether or not he will be able to recover it, in the event it is captured.

White must not attempt to win a Pawn with 5 PxP, PxP;
6 NxP. For Black continues with 6 . . . NxN and wins a
piece! 7 BxQ, B-N5*ch;* 8 Q-Q2, BxQ*ch;* 9 KxB, KxB.

5 . . . .   B-K2

The best post for the Bishop, since it relieves the pin
on Black's King Knight. On Q3, the Bishop is aggressively
disposed but in a somewhat incongruous position. For Black's
role is to defend successfully and break loose only after he
has achieved equality and freedom of action. Black must
first solve the problem of the "problem Bishop."

6 N-B3 . . . .

Since Black's King Knight is no longer pinned, there is
no point to swapping the Queen Pawn, except to revert to
the Exchange Variation. As already mentioned, the Exchange
Variation frees Black's problem Bishop. It does not matter,
in this instance, that Black's Knight is posted at Q2 and blocks
the problem Bishop. This block is only temporary.

The text move is in line with the plan of development,
to put pressure on the center.

6 . . . .   O-O

Black completes his King-side development, establishing
a new haven for his King.

7 R-B1 . . . .

White elects to put the Rook on a file which will be
opened, sooner or later. This is what is technically called a
positional move.

7 . . . .   P-B3

Black reinforces the Queen Pawn so that Black's King Knight will be able to move, when necessary.

8 B-Q3 . . . .

White brings out his last minor piece and puts it on a square which bears in the general direction of the Black Monarch, for future reference.

A résumé of the position at this point discloses the following advantages in White's favor. (1) White has a better grip on the center. (2) White enjoys greater freedom of action. (3) Black must solve the problem of the "problem Bishop."

8 . . . .   PxP

The first step in Black's over-all plan to solve all of his difficulties. The exchange vacates Black's Q4 and enables Black to use that square to relieve pressure and simplify the forces by exchanges.

9 BxP   N-Q4

Black virtually forces the exchange of White's Queen Bishop; the second step in the plan.

10 BxB   QxB
11 O-O   . . . .

White's development goes on apace.

11 . . . .   NxN

The third step in the plan. Soon the idea of how Black expects to free his problem Bishop will become clear.

12 RxN   . . . .

To exercise pressure on the Queen Bishop file and also, in some contingencies, to swing the Rook over to the King-side of the board, after P-K4.

12 . . . .   P-K4

The fourth step. Now the original diagonal of Black's Queen Bishop—closed on Black's second move—is open once again.

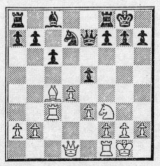

From here on, Black should be able to ward off any on-slaught against his King, with exacting defense.

Two suggested continuations are:

(1) 13 PxP, NxP; 14 NxN, QxN; 15 P-B4!, Q-K5!; 16 B-N3, B-B4; 17 Q-R5, P-KN3; 18 Q-R6, QR-Q1; 19 B-B2, Q-Q4; 20 P-K4, BxP, with about even chances.

White has a strong continuation in 21 R-KR3.

(2) 13 Q-B2, P-K5; 14 N-Q2, N-B3; 15 R-B1, B-B4; 16 P-B4, QR-Q1; 17 P-QR3, P-KR4; 18 P-QN4, P-KN3; 19 Q-N3, R-Q2, with even chances.

Conclusions

Of all the openings at White's command, those beginning with the move 1 P-Q4 grant White the longest-lasting pressure. True, Black is able to hold his own with correct defense. But the onus of exactitude rests with the defender.

Chess Movie

MOVE CLIMACTERIC

THE Orthodox Defense to the Queen Gambit Declined is a low-geared starter. About midway during hostilities, it shifts to second gear and then quickly to high. At a whirlwind pace, Dr. Max Euwe defeats Sir George Thomas in the memorable contest of Hastings, 1934–5. The game begins with: *1* P-QB4, P-K3; *2* N-QB3, P-Q4; *3* P-Q4, N-KB3 (*see diagram No. 1*).

1 There follows: *4* B-N5, B-K2; *5* P-K3, O-O; *6* N-B3, QN-Q2; *7* R-B1, P-B3. Each player sticks to the accredited line, reaching the book position by slight transpositions in sequence. The moves are more or less automatic, with years of logic and reason engraved into every turn.

2 Still the players keep to the tried and true. So there follows: *8* B-Q3, PxP; *9* BxP, N-Q4; *10* BxB, QxB; *11* O-O, NxN; *12* RxN, P-K4. Sir George at last solves the problem of his "problem Bishop." He has not yet, however, resolved the bigger problem—the further course of the game.

3 Euwe continues with 13 NxP, and a general exchange ensues: *13 . . . NxN; 14 PxN, QxP.* Then Euwe signals an attack with *15 P-B4.* The King Bishop Pawn is full of portent. It reaches out in the direction of the Black King. How shall Sir George stave off the impending onslaught?

4 Sir George retreats his Queen, with *15 . . . Q-K2,* and he errs in not preventing the further advance of the King Bishop Pawn. Now *16 P-B5* is the move, Black's natural development is subdued. His Bishop, once more, must find a way out. To boot, Black's King-side Pawn structure is menaced.

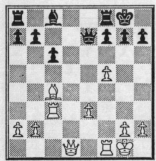

5 Sir George counters with *16 . . . P-QN4*—a wing demonstration. He now hopes to divert his noted adversary's attention from his own King. At the same time, he creates an exit for his Bishop. Euwe retreats: *17 B-N3,* and *17 . . . P-N5* follows. Now comes the initial break-through. *18 P-B6* is the move.

6 Sir George captures: *18 . . . PxP,* and Euwe follows up with *19 QRxP.* A Pawn or so, when the King is exposed, does not add up. Sir George plays *19 . . . QxPch,* and Euwe retreats, with *20 K-R1.* At long last, the problem Bishop enters the fray, with *20 . . . B-N2.* Both sides are now alerted.

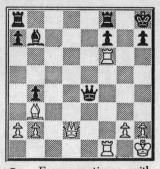

7 There follows: *21 QRxP, Q-K5.* Black focuses his attention on the White King. Euwe defends, with *22 Q-Q2* and, at the same time, prepares to swing his Queen into action against the opposing King. There follows: *22 . . . K-R1,* and each side appraises the open King Knight file enviously.

8 Euwe continues with *23 BxP.* No enemy Rook will occupy the King Knight file if he can prevent it. And Sir George counters with *23 . . . QR-B1.* Now Euwe defends with *24 R/6-B2.* Attack and defend—that is the order of play. Now the question is: who is going to break out next—and where?

9 Sir George temporizes by *24 . . . QR-Q1,* and Euwe penetrates, with *25 Q-N5.* For a moment all is calm. Sir George seizes the opportunity to utilize his Rook for what appears double duty —attack and defense. *25 . . . R-Q3* is the move. Little does he realize that the climax is at hand.

10 This is the calm before the storm. With one fell move, the game is about to end. *26 B-Q5* is the move. It spells *finis.* Everything is under fire at once. The Queen, the Rook, the Bishop and the hapless monarch. No mortal could withstand such a blow. Sir George is but mortal after all. He resigns.

12

Réti Opening

A HYPERMODERN OPENING

During the past few decades, brand new ideas have developed in opening play. The fight for control of the center —the paramount issue in modern openings—has been given a new twist. A new school of thought has been born. Whereas, in the modern school, the skirmish waxes openly and merrily for domination of the mid-section of the playing field from the very first move, in the new school—the hypermodern school—the contest for center control takes the form of long distance, sniping, wing attacks on the opposing center.

The modernist will not give ground in the center. The hypermodernist, on the other hand, will permit, induce or even provoke his opponent into taking early control of the center. This seems rather strange. For, if it is important to control the center—and the modernist and the hypermodernist agree that it is—why should the *ne plus ultra* school of thought deliberately present to the adversary what is so valuable? The reasons for this, even though apparently obscure, are really pointed. What the hypermodernist really grants to the opponent is the occupation of the center. The occupied field then sets up as a ready target. And the hypermodernist shoots. His long-term plan is to demolish the occupied enemy field and take over the vital terrain, while he is still strong and the opposing center is in shambles.

This is the new idea. And Réti's opening is part and parcel of it.

The opening begins with *1 N-KB3*, attributed to Zukertort for popularizing it. *1* N-KB3 is recorded in Lopez, 1561, and the first known game wherein it was essayed was dated 1845.

The Réti arises as follows:

1 N-KB3 . . . .

The first move, of itself, does not have any exemplary significance; it is purely noncommittal and may transpose into the regular lines of the Queen's Pawn Game. White's second move, in conjunction with the first, gives the opening the hypermodern turn. This is called the Réti, after the late grandmaster, Richard Réti, one of the disciples of the hyper-modern school.

The hypermodern idea, like all ideas, is excellent—when it succeeds. When it fails because the opponent has been presented with the center and all it portends, the hypermodernist is left in a sorry state.

The development of the Knight on the first move does not, of itself, indicate what course White will pursue. It might be a prelude to the Queen's Pawn Opening or even a King's Pawn game, in some contingencies. Insofar as White's intention is momentarily concealed, the move is meritorious. On purely theoretical grounds, the move is also good. The Knight strikes at two important central squares, Q4 and K5.

1 . . . . P-Q4

At this point and later on, the order of moves lends itself to transpositions. For instance, Black might also play 1 . . . N-KB3. Or he might begin with 1 . . . P-K3 or 1 . . . P-QB4. In the latter cases, White may choose to convert the opening into the French Defense or the Sicilian Defense by playing 2 P-K4. Insofar as Black's Pawn at Q4 strikes at two important squares, K5 and QB5, the move is good.

2 P-B4 . . . .

The move which characterizes the Réti. It is a direct assault against Black's staunch Queen Pawn.

2 . . . . P-QB3

Defending the Queen Pawn and maintaining Pawn symmetry, if White should exchange. At this point, Black again has a choice of replies:

(1) 2 . . . PxP. For an effective counter-pattern. The line might run as follows: 2 . . . PxP; 3 N-R3, P-QB4; 4 NxP, N-QB3; 5 P-KN3, P-B3; 6 B-N2, P-K4; 7 P-Q3, B-K3; 8 O-O,

KN-K2; 9 KN-Q2, N-Q4. Black maintains a strong grip on the center with excellent prospects.

Observe that Black does not capture the Pawn with a view to retaining it. With correct play, it is not possible to hold the Pawn. Moreover, an attempt to hold it weakens the Black position.

After 2 . . . PxP, however, White may continue with 3 P-K3 and lead into the Queen's Gambit Accepted, thus: 3 . . . N-KB3; 4 BxP, P-K3; 5 O-O, P-B4; 6 P-Q4. In this line, opinion favors White.

(2) 2 . . . P-Q5. To establish a bridgehead in enemy territory. This variation is in line with White's plan of inducing occupation of the center so that the occupied field will set up as a target. It is double-edged, however. For, if Black can successfully maintain the advanced Pawn, White will be cramped. If the bridgehead and its props can be battered down, however, White will gain the advantage. The line might run as follows: 2 . . . P-Q5; 3 P-K3, P-QB4; 4 PxP, PxP; 5 P-KN3, N-QB3; 6 B-N2, P-KN3; 7 P-Q3, B-N2; 8 O-O, P-K4; 9 R-K1, P-B3. Although White enjoys a Queen-side Pawn majority, Black's position is freer, and Black can maintain the bridgehead.

(3) 2 . . . P-K3. The routine, neutral development. The line might run as follows: 3 P-KN3, N-KB3; 4 B-N2, B-Q3; 5 P-N3, O-O; 6 O-O, QN-Q2; 7 B-N2, P-B3; 8 P-Q4, N-K5; 9 QN-Q2, P-KB4; 10 NxN, BPxN; 11 N-K1, N-B3; 12 P-B3, B-Q2; 13 PxKP, NxP, with about even chances.

3 P-QN3 . . . .

To defend the unguarded Bishop Pawn, which is now in danger of being captured. At the same time, the move makes way for the fianchetto of the Queen Bishop—the hypermodern idea of eyeing the center from the wings.

3 . . . . N-B3

A good developing move which strikes at the center.

4 P-N3   . . . .

Making ready for the fianchetto of the King Bishop—also in line with the hypermodern idea of bearing down on the center from a distance. The pressure which the White Bishops will exercise on the bias is the highlight of the over-all plan.

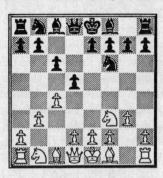

4 . . . .   **B-B4**

In the Queen Pawn openings, Black, as a rule, is saddled with the "problem Bishop." For the Queen Bishop is tied down to guarding Black's Queen Knight Pawn. So long as White does not have ready access to Black's Queen Knight Pawn—the usual method is Q-N3 for White—there is no reason not to develop the Queen Bishop. Hence it is brought out before Black locks the diagonal with . . . P-K3. Now the Bishop will participate in the play, actively.

5 B-KN2 QN-Q2

Bringing out additional force and intending 6 . . . P-K4.

6 B-N2   . . . .

Preventing the opposing . . . P-K4 and dominating White's K5 via long distance.

6 . . . .   **P-K3**

Black must content himself with moving the King Pawn one square for the present. Should he play 6 . . . Q-B2, with the idea of playing the Pawn up two squares, he will find that his Queen is misplaced, after a few moves. White will soon place his Queen Rook with telling effect on QB1 and this will be the equivalent of an indirect frontal assault on the Queen. White is also at liberty to play his Queen Pawn to Q4 and prevent Black from playing . . . P-K4. This, however, is out of the spirit of the hypermodern opening. Moreover, it cedes Black's K5 to Black.

7 **O-O** . . . .

Continuing the development.

7 . . . .   **B-Q3**

To prepare for . . . P-K4 and also to allow for a good square for Black's Queen at K2. That is why the text move is superior to . . . B-K2. At K2, Black's Queen cannot be molested.

8 **P-Q3** . . . .

White also prepares for P-K4. The text move is the first step.

8 . . . .   **O-O!**

Because of technical reasons, 8 . . . P-K4 would expedite White's reply of P-K4. Thus, if *8* . . . P-K4; *9* P-K4, and Black dare not win a Pawn with *9* . . . PxKP; *10* PxP, NxP, for *11* N-R4 will win a piece for White.

9 **QN-Q2** . . . .

Continuing the development and reinforcing the K4 square for the eventual P-K4.

9 . . . .   **P-K4**

Now Black has occupied the center. Black's center Pawns are supposed to set up as a target—according to hypermodern theory. Unfortunately, however, they do not. For it is difficult for White to put additional force against the opposing center.

10 **PxP**   . . . .

In order to open the Queen Bishop file for use by White's Queen Rook.

10 . . . .   **PxP**

11 **R-B1**   **Q-K2**

Black's development seems to be sound.

A game Réti—Emanuel Lasker, New York, 1924, continued as follows: *12* R-B2, P-QR4; *13* P-QR4, P-R3; *14* Q-R1, KR-K1; *15* KR-B1, B-R2; *16* N-B1, N-B4.

Réti then sacrificed the exchange with *17* RxN but did not obtain sufficient compensation.

Conclusions

The Réti system has infused new life into opening play. When first introduced, it met with remarkable success, mainly because adequate parrying, defensive formations were unknown. At present, there is no known way which leads to an advantage for White. Moreover, Black enjoys more latitude in this system than against the usual Queen Pawn Game.

Chess Movie

READY FOR THE RETI?

W<small>HEN</small> pure ideas clash, only a fine line separates success from failure. Here grandmaster Kashdan is the hypermodernist against the modernist Horowitz, in the USCF Open of Philadelphia, 1936. The game begins with *1* N-KB3, P-Q4; *2* P-B4, P-Q5; *3* P-KN3, P-QB4; *4* B-N2, N-QB3; *5* O-O, P-K4 (*see diagram No. 1*).

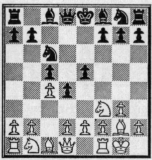 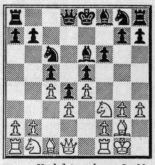

1 Black has usurped the center, with White's knowledge and consent. The question arises, is the center field a ready target? There follows *6* P-K4, B-N5; *7* P-KR3, B-K3; *8* P-Q3, P-B3. To all appearances, Black's wedge-shaped Pawn formation is secure. But White has his own ideas.

2 Kashdan plays *9* N-R3. He intends to swing the Knight to B2 and concentrate on a break at his QN4—The first step in undermining the Pawn array. Then comes *9* . . . Q-Q2; *10* K-R2, P-KN4; *11* N-B2, P-KR4. Black's target is White's King. A bit of speculation is involved.

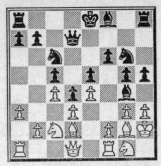

3 White retreats *12* N-N1, and Black follows with *12 . . .* KN-K2. The Knight is headed for the vicinity of the White King. There follows *13* B-Q2, lining up on QN4. Black replies *13 . . .* N-N3. Now comes *14* P-R3, B-N5. Black wishes to force open a file leading to the opposing monarch.

4 White captures *15* PxB, and Black recaptures *15 . . .* PxP*ch*. Now White closes the file by returning a piece with *16* N-R3. White prefers a slow, peaceful game, where he can demolish the opposing center in good time. Black has other ideas. *16 . . .* N-B5 is the move, and it poses difficult problems.

5 White has little choice. He captures the Knight with *17* PxN, and then comes *17 . . .* KPxP; *18* P-B3, PxN; *19* B-R1, N-K4; *20* Q-K2, B-Q3; *21* R-KN1, O-O-O. The battle waxes furious. Black is a piece behind, but with two Pawns to the good and a powerful attack. Can White survive?

6 White attempts a diversion with *22* P-N4. Black parries with *22 . . .* P-N3, and White continues with *23* P-R4. There follows *23 . . .* QR-N1; *24* P-R5, P-N5. Each player is racing to get in heavy blows against the hostile King. And right now it looks like a toss-up. It is White's turn.

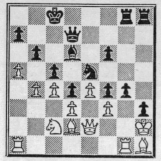

7 The fast-moving action places both players on the alert. White plays 25 BxP, and the game continues 25 . . . NxPch; 26 BxN, BxBch; 27 K-R1, P-N6; 28 RxP, RxR. Now Black is the exchange to the good. But he must reckon with White's assault; his own seems stymied. Can he contain the counterattack?

8 White opens the line of his own Rook's battery with 29 RPxP, and Black ignores the apparent danger by playing 29 . . . KR-N1. Now White captures 30 PxRP. For a moment it appears that all is over. A new Queen is the menace. Black captures, however, 30 . . . QxP, and the scene changes.

9 The Queen is immune from capture on account of mate! Now White combines to simplify the position. He plays 31 B-N4ch, and there follows 31 . . . R/6xB; 32 QxRch, RxQ; 33 RxQ. After all, material is even. But White is in a mating net. Black plays 33 . . . R-N7 and draws the net tighter.

10 White retreats his unguarded Knight: 34 N-K1, and there follows 34 . . . R-KB7, closing in. White plays 35 K-N1 and Black counters with 35 . . . P-R7ch, pinning down the monarch. White captures 36 KxR, and Black plays 36 . . . P-R8(Q). The game is over. The Queen decides.

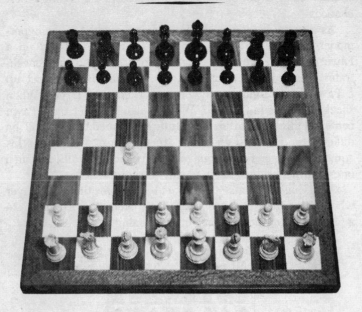

English Opening

ANOTHER HYPERMODERN OPENING

THE English Opening—once known as the Queen's Bishop's Pawn Game—is so called after Staunton who adopted it in the match between England and France, 1843.

With *1* P-QB4, the English Opening is a Sicilian Defense in reverse, with White having a move in hand. If the Sicilian is tenable for Black, it should definitely be good for White, with a tempo to spare. At least, that is the underlying theory of the opening. As Réti says, however, in *Masters of the Chess-*

*board,** such a policy may be too passive for White's best chances.

As commonly played, the English is a product of the hyper-modern school. So White makes no attempt to build up a Pawn center in the early stages of play. Instead, he concentrates on speedy development, encouraging Black to set up a Pawn center which may become fixed as a target. When Black does not fall in line, White's plan is to set up a Pawn center of his own, after he is fully developed, which will be difficult for Black to challenge. In that case, White uses his square Q5, as a focal point around which to rally his men or establish a bridgehead in enemy territory.

The English lends itself to easy transpositions. A player whose repertoire is large may easily steer the English into a favorable variation of some other opening.

The English arises as follows:

1 P-QB4 . . . .

This move constitutes the English Opening. The Pawn at QB4 strikes at the central square, Q5, and the less important one, QN5. The advance of the Bishop Pawn also releases White's Queen for future action.

The eventual pattern which evolves from the initial move depends, in a large measure, on Black's choice of defense.

1 . . . . P-K4

* Réti, R., MASTERS OF THE CHESSBOARD, N. Y., *McGraw-Hill.*

As a general rule, and this is a case in point, it is good for Black to play . . . P-K4 at the first convenient opportunity. Black's King Pawn now strikes at Black's Q5, an important central square, and Black's KB5, a near central square. The advance of the King Pawn, moreover, releases Black's Queen and his King Bishop for future action.

Momentarily, Black appears to have the more dominating position. This appearance is somewhat of an illusion, since White has the first move and is able, at will, to swap off Black's King Pawn.

For players versed in the intricacies of the defense to the Queen Pawn, *1* . . . P-K3 is apt to transpose into that opening. In such case, White can avoid the Queen Pawn only by continuing with *2* P-K4. Then, by playing *2* . . . P-Q4, Black obtains a favorable position, thus: *3* KPxP, KPxP; *4* PxP, N-KB3. With correct play, Black recovers the Queen Pawn, and White remains with an isolated Queen Pawn. Of course, Black can play *4* . . . QxP, in this line, and avoid any speculation as to the recovery of the Pawn. Then, however, White gains an important tempo by *5* N-QB3, attacking the Black Queen.

2 N-QB3 . . . .

A good developing move, bearing on the center and particularly on Q5.

2 . . . . N-KB3

A good developing move, bearing on the center and neutralizing the effect of White's Queen Knight.

3 N-B3 . . . .

Again, a good developing move, bearing on the center and particularly on Black's King Pawn.

3 . . . . N-B3

Defending the King Pawn and maintaining the delicate balance in the center.

Observe that the natural *3* . . . P-K5 loses a Pawn: *4* N-

KN5, Q-K2; 5 Q-B2, and Black has no way of reinforcing the King Pawn.

The Four Knights' Game of the English.

4 P-Q4 . . . .

The most logical line. In the actual Sicilian Defense, Black has a difficult time enforcing . . . P-Q4. When he does, however, he achieves at least certain equality. With the move in hand, White has no trouble battering down Black's King Pawn. After White's Queen Pawn and Black's King Pawn are swapped off, Black must still equalize the pressure on the center, exerted by the White Bishop Pawn.

The slower, positional continuation leads to no advantage for White. For example, *4* P-KN3, P-Q4; *5* PxP, NxP; *6* B-N2, N-N3; *7* O-O, B-K2; *8* P-Q3, O-O; *9* P-QR3, P-B4; *10* P-QN4,

B-B3; *11* B-N2, Q-K2; *12* N-Q2, R-Q1; *13* P-N5, N-R4; *14* Q-B2, P-B4; *15* N-R4, B-K3; *16* B-B3, N-N6 with the better game for Black (Santasiere—Horowitz, New York, 1939).

$$4 \ldots \quad \textbf{PxP}$$

Black can attempt to maintain the King Pawn by *4 . . . P-K5*. With best play, however, White obtains a positional advantage, although the line is beset with traps. Thus, if *4 . . . P-K5; 5* N-Q2, NxP; *6* KNxP, N-K3; *7* P-KN3, NxN; *8* NxN, B-N5ch; *9* B-Q2, BxBch; *10* QxB, O-O; *11* B-N2, P-Q3; *12* O-O, B-Q2; *13* N-B3, B-B3; *14* N-Q5, and White enjoys command of the center and greater freedom for his forces.

The trappy line runs as follows: *4 . . .* P-K5; *5* N-KN5, P-KR3!; *6* KNxKP, NxN; *7* NxN, Q-R5; *8* Q-Q3, P-Q4; *9* PxP, N-N5; *10* Q-N1, B-KB4; *11* N-Q6ch, PxN!; *12* QxB, P-KN3; *13* Q-N1, R-B1, and there is nought to be done about . . . N-B7.

$$5 \ \textbf{NxP} \qquad \textbf{B-N5}$$

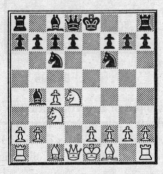

Black pins White's Queen Knight in order to lessen the pressure on White's Q5. This move practically commits Black to the exchange of Bishop for Knight. Black obtains compensation, however, in doubling and isolating White's Pawns.

$$6 \ \textbf{B-N5} \quad \ldots$$

By the same token, White pins Black's King Knight in order to increase the pressure on Q5. At the same time, the pin is an-

noying and restricts the freedom of Black's King Knight and
Queen.

6 . . . . P-KR3

"Putting the question" to the Bishop. The point of the move
is to break the pin.

7 B-R4 . . . .

Maintaining the pin. Clearly, any other Bishop moves are
pointless.

7 . . . . BxNch

Since Black is more or less committed to this exchange, he
might as well make it while he is certain that White's Pawn position will suffer. Otherwise White defends his Queen Knight
by R-B1, after which . . . BxN is less efficacious.

8 PxB   N-K4

Black follows up his 6th move, in conformity with the idea
of breaking the pin on his King Knight.

9 P-K3 . . . .

To defend the unguarded Pawn.

9 . . . . P-Q3

A necessary interpolation, sooner or later, in order to prevent White from playing P-B5. That move would give freer range to White's King Bishop and, at the same time, assist White in getting rid of his doubled Pawn.

10 B-K2   N-N3

Breaking the pin, at last. Observe the three steps involved in this process: . . . P-KR3, . . . N-K4 and . . . N-N3.

11 B-N3   N-K5

Black aims to rid White of his two Bishops before he can consolidate his position with P-B3 and P-K4.

12 Q-B2   . . . .

Defending the unguarded Bishop Pawn and, in turn, attacking the aggressively posted Black Knight.

$$12 \ldots . \quad \text{Q-K2}$$

Since White cannot avoid the exchange of Bishop for Knight, Black has no present need to pare off and give up the centrally posted Knight.

$$13 \ \text{B-Q3} \quad \ldots .$$

This move was played by the late world champion, Dr. Emanuel Lasker. After 13 O-O, there is an element of danger in the following continuation: 13 . . . P-KR4; 14 B-Q3, NxB; 15 RPxN, N-K4; 16 B-K2, P-R5.

$$13 \ldots . \quad \text{NxB}$$
$$14 \ \text{RPxN} \quad \text{N-K4}$$

The position is considered even. The weak White Queen-side structure rules in favor of Black, and White's centrally located forces favor him.

Conclusions

In most of the book lines of the English Opening, White enjoys the advantage. Only by accurate play is Black able to equalize. The onus of accuracy is with the defender, and this is not a burden lightly to be discounted. There is every reason, moreover, to believe that White's play can be refined and improved, in which case Black's burden will be even greater.

Chess Movie

THREATS IN ALL DIRECTIONS

PARADOXICALLY, a weakened Queen-side can incur a loss on the opposite wing, as is masterfully demonstrated in the following Fine game. In the U. S. Championship, New York, 1936, Reuben Fine opens hostilities with Weaver Adams (Black): *1* P-QB4, P-K4; *2* N-KB3, N-QB3; *3* N-B3; N-B3; *4* P-K4 (*see diagram No. 1*).

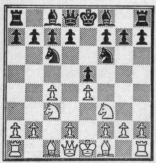

1 Fine chooses a Nimzo-vich idea, departing from the more usual *4* P-Q4. Adams replies *4* . . . B-B4 (since *5* NxP, NxN; *6* P-Q4, B-N5; *7* PxN, NxP leaves White's Pawns weak). There follows: *5* B-K2, P-Q3; *6* O-O, and Black now makes the excellent move, *6* . . . B-KN5! (preventing *7* P-Q4).

2 So the game continues with *7* P-Q3, O-O; after which White pins Black's King Knight, *8* B-N5, and Black reacts with *8* . . . P-KR3 (hoping for *9* B-R4, P-KN4; *10* B-N3, N-KR4 to gain the two Bishops). White rejoins *9* B-K3. (Now Black misses the equalizer: *9* . . . BxN; *10* BxB, N-Q5!)

3 Instead, he plays *9 . . . B-N3?* and White prepares for an eventual P-KB4, by *10 K-R1.* Black still ignores the equalizer and decides to get in the "break" first. There follows: *10 . . . N-KR4; 11 N-Q5, P-B4; 12 PxP,* and Black's maneuver has left him with the inferior game.

4 Adams now sees he must permit P-Q4 (as *12 . . . RxP?; 13 BxB, RPxB; 14 N-K3* loses for him). Hence *12 . . . BxP* and a general exchange follows: *13 P-Q4, PxP; 14 Nx QP, NxN; 15 QBxN, BxB; 16 QxB.* Adams then returns his Knight, *16 . . . N-B3,* and seemingly he has simplified the game safely.

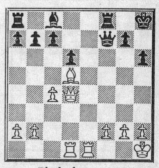

5 Actually, Black's Queenside is weak, and White now builds his game to a win on that account. There follows: *17 B-B3, K-R1; 18 N-K3, B-B1; 19 QR-Q1, Q-K2; 20 KR-K1, Q-B2; 21 N-Q5.* And Black is constrained to exchange: *21 . . . NxN; 22 BxN* (as *21 . . . B-K3?* loses to *22 NxP!*).

6 Black dare not capture *22 . . . QxP* because of *23 R-K8!* So there follows: *22 . . . Q-N3; 23 R-K7, P-B3; 24 B-B3* (White could win a Pawn by *24 B-K4, B-B4; 25 BxB, RxB; 26 RxP,* but the position then is drawish). Now Black sees *24 . . . B-R6* loses to *25 QxQP, R-B3; 26 Q-N3.*

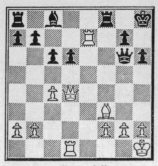

7 So there follows: *24 . . . R-B3; 25 R/1-K1, K-R2?* (Now *25 . . . B-R6* is Black's sole hope: *26 B-K4, B-B4; 27 P-B3,* and White must win a Pawn but faces a very difficult ending with Queens and two Rooks on each side.) As is, White now scores: *26 B-R5!* is the move which upsets the apple cart.

8 Pressure on Black's weak Queen-side Pawns has restrained Black; but now the action switches drastically to the King-side. (*26 . . . QxB?* 27 QxR will not do.) Hence *26 . . . Q-N4; 27 P-KR4, Q-B5* follows. (Danger lies in *27 . . . Q-B4; 28 B-K2, Q-N3; 29 P-R5, Q-N4; 30 R-K8* and *31 B-Q3ch* next!)

9 But White now makes his point: *28 QxQ, Rx Q; 29 P-KN3!* He'll double Rooks on the 7th if Black retreats. Black takes: *29 . . . RxQBP* (as *29 . . . Rx-KBP* leads to a mating net: *30 R-K8, P-QN3; 31 K-N1!* R-B3; *32 R/1-K7* and B-K2-Q3ch). There follows: *30 R-K8, P-QN3; 31 B-B7!*

10 White threatens P-R5 and B-N6 mate! Black covers: *31 . . . R-KN5,* vainly, as then comes: *32 P-R5, B-N2; 33 RxR, BxR; 34 R-K8,* with threats in all directions. (On *34 . . . B-N2,* White wins by *35 B-N8ch, K-R1; 36 B-K6ch.*) Black resigns. Even at the end, his Queen-side ruins his King-side.

14

Alekhine's Defense

HYPERMODERNISM IN DEFENSE

THE last word in hypermodernism is Alekhine's Defense. In this weird ripost to *1* P-K4, Black brings out his Knight to KB3 on the very first move, where it can be mauled and pummeled and driven clear across the board to what appears to be innocuous desuetude. Yet Black's play is not buffoonery; it is purposeful. It is a designed attempt to lure an onrush of enemy Pawns and set them up as fixed targets. In doing so, Black completely cedes the center. This is, however, the essence of hypermodernism.

Alekhine's Defense is named after late world champion Alexander Alekhine, who introduced it to master play at Budapest, 1921. Long before this time, it made an occasional appearance, and its debut can be traced to the International Handicap Tournament of London, 1862. In the game, Anderssen–Pearson, at odds of a Knight, play proceeded *1* P-K4, N-KB3. This provoked two question marks from annotator von Gotschall, who went on to say that *1* . . . N-KB3 must lose quickly, even at Knight odds. Schallopp's seventh edition of Bilguer's *Handbuch* * had a kindlier word for Black's enigmatic first move. "If you are playing an inferior player," it reads, "you can try *1* P-K4, N-KB3; *2* P-K5, N-N1, as your opponent will often not be in position to prevent the break-up of his advanced center."

So it goes. Ideas, frowned upon one hundred years ago, enjoy the limelight today. Others that were significantly prominent have fallen from grace and are looked upon askance. *Chess marches on!*

The defense arises as follows:

1 P-K4   N-KB3

Black's move is forcefully provocative. The Knight attacks the King Pawn. Hence White must defend or advance.

The defense of the Pawn with *2* N-QB3 or *2* P-Q3 is hardly within the spirit of rebuttal. In a game of chess, nevertheless, the spirit is to be counted lightly. If the move produces a plus, it is to be played; if it leads to equality or a minus, it is to be discarded.

* Schallopp, E., *Handbuch des Schachspiels*, Leipzig, *Veit & Comp.*

2 N-QB3 fails mainly because Black is able to continue with
. . . P-Q4, without loss of time. This move is usually barred to
Black. For, after *1* P-K4, P-Q4; *2* PxP, Black must recapture
with the Queen. Then *3* N-QB3 gains a vital tempo for White.
Here, if *1* P-K4, N-KB3; *2* N-QB3, P-Q4; *3* PxP, NxP and Black
has nothing to fear.

The line beginning with 2 N-QB3 might run as follows:
2 . . . P-Q4; *3* PxP, NxP; *4* B-B4, P-K3; *5* N-B3, P-QB4; *6* O-O,
B-K2; *7* P-Q4, NxN; *8* PxN, O-O; *9* N-K5, Q-B2, with about
even chances.

In this line, if *3* P-K5, Black can equalize with *3* . . . P-Q5
or *3* . . . KN-Q2.

The passive 2 P-Q3, however, conceals tricky tactical plays
which must be parried exactly. A game, Nimzóvich—Alekhine,
New York, 1927, went as follows: *2* P-Q3, P-K4; *3* P-KB4,
N-B3; *4* PxP, QNxP; *5* N-KB3, NxNch; *6* QxN, P-Q4; *7* P-K5,
Q-K2; *8* P-Q4, N-K5; *9* B-Q3, Q-R5ch; *10* P-N3, Q-N5; *11*
N-Q2, QxQ; *12* NxQ, with equality.

2 **P-K5** . . . .

In view of the above, White advances his Pawn and attacks
the Knight out of compulsion and choice. Since the Pawn cannot be defended to advantage, it must advance. Since White
gains time in the advance, he is satisfied.

2 . . . . **N-Q4**

All part of the grand hypermodern plan. The Knight goes where it may be directly attacked again in order to lure onwards White's center Pawns.

3 P-QB4 . . . .

White accepts the challenge. He is willing to be lured on.

From here on, the issue is whether the time gained by advancing the Pawns at Black's expense is equal to the minimal inherent weakness in the center Pawn structure. So fine is the line drawn.

Observe that it is important to drive Black's Knight from the center field. This can be done in another way: 3 N-QB3, NxN; 4 NPxN, P-Q3; 5 P-KB4, P-KN3; 6 N-B3, B-N2; 7 P-Q4, P-QB4; 8 B-Q3, O-O; 9 O-O, Q-B2; 10 Q-K1, BPxP; 11 BPxP, N-B3; 12 P-B3, N-R4. The position is equal.

3 . . . . N-N3

4 P-Q4 . . . .

White enjoys what appears to be an imposing center. Black has other ideas about the strength of the center.

An interesting alternative here is 4 P-B5, N-Q4; 5 N-QB3. After 5 . . . NxN; 6 NPxN, P-Q3, Black can equalize. Also in this line, 5 B-QB4 develops into a lively gambit.

4 . . . .   **P-Q3**

The first thrust at the opposing center. Curiously, 4 . . . N-B3 loses a piece! 5 P-Q5, NxKP; 6 P-B5, N/3-B5; 7 Q-Q4, threatening P-KB4 and P-QN3, each of which forces the abandonment of one of the Knights.

5 PxP   . . . .

The all-out acceptance of Black's plan is 5 P-B4. In that case, White obtains a commanding array of center Pawns.

Whether they are strong or weak, however, is the question. In any event, after 5 P-B4, Black enjoys quite a lot of counterplay, and White must continue accurately. This line might go as follows: 5 P-B4, PxP; 6 BPxP, N-B3; 7 B-K3, B-B4; 8 N-QB3, P-K3; 9 N-B3, N-N5; 10 R-B1, P-B4; 11 B-K2, PxP; 12 NxP, B-N3; 13 P-QR3, N-B3; 14 NxN, PxN; 15 QxQch, KxQ. Despite Black's weak Queen-side Pawn structure, the chances are level. White has no easy way of exploiting the weaknesses and Black enjoys a free an l easy development for all his forces.

Of course, Black can also go wrong. For instance, if 9 . . . B-K2 (instead of 9 . . . N-N5), White gets a terrific onslaught by 10 P-Q5, PxP; 11 PxP, N-N5; 12 N-Q4, B-N3; 13 B-N5ch, K-B1; 14 O-O. The threat of 15 N-K6ch gains more time, and Black's position is extremely critical.

The text move consolidates White's position and maintains the advantage of a stable center.

$$5 . . . . \quad \text{KPxP}$$

5 . . . BPxP is an alternative which keeps the Pawn position unbalanced and consequently creates greater winning and losing chances for both sides. White, however, can obtain an excellent bind on the position with correct play, thus: 6 N-KB3, P-N3; 7 B-K2, B-N2; 8 N-R3! N-B3; 9 P-Q5, N-K4; 10 N-Q4. The advance of P-KB4 compels a retreat and cramps Black. Moreover, Black cannot free his game easily by . . . P-K3, as, after PxP, PxP, his center is weak.

Observe the unique move of 8 N-R3. The immediate purpose of the move is to defend the Queen Bishop Pawn, so that when Black plays 8 . . . N-QB3, White can immediately play 9 P-Q5, N-K4; 10 N-Q4, and not worry about exchanging his King Knight. He might have to—if the QBP were not defended.

6	N-KB3	B-K2
7	B-K2	O-O
8	O-O	B-N5

9 N-R3

All the foregoing moves are good developing moves. White's last, however, is unusual. Oddly enough, it is not made with the intention of defending the Queen Bishop Pawn. For Black does not threaten 9 . . . BxN; *10* BxB, NxP. In such an instance, White could reply BxP and win the exchange. The reason for 9 N-R3 becomes clear later.

9	**B-B3**	
10 **P-QN3**	**N-B3**	

11 **N-B2** . . . .

Observe the maneuver of White's Queen Knight.

$$
\begin{array}{lll}
11 & \ldots & \text{R-K1} \\
12 & \text{B-N2} & \text{Q-Q2} \\
13 & \text{N-K3!} & \ldots
\end{array}
$$

The final destination of the Knight.

White is for choice. On the surface, Black appears to have an adequate development. The fact is, Black has just about reached his maximum development and can hardly improve his position. White, on the other hand, has a flexible position. His future plan may be to play *14* Q-Q2, followed by P-Q5 and N-Q4. Then, he will be in command of greater terrain, which he should be able to exploit and capitalize.

Conclusions

Alekhine's Defense, which has all the earmarks of arrogant nonsense, is really a comparatively sound weapon in the hands of those looking for a lively encounter. While White's prospects are brighter, with sound play, the chance for error is greater than in most other defenses.

Chess Movie

OLD WHAM IN NEW BATTLES

Slow, plodding, positional Hypermodernism tussles with old Modernism. A long, drawn-out contest is in store. Tactics makes an entry. The scene changes and the play is over. U. S. Championship Tournament, New York, 1942, produced this contest between Horowitz and Seidman. Follow the game "movie style." *1* P-K4, N-KB3; *2* P-K5, N-Q4; *3* P-QB4, N-N3; *4* P-Q4, P-Q3. (*See diagram No. 1.*)

1 White plays the Four Pawn game. There follows 5 P-B4. Black counters with the infrequent 5 . . . P-N3. His King Bishop is destined for a wing development, from which point of vantage it will bear directly on the opposing center. 6 N-QB3, B-N2 are next in order, reaching diagram No. 2.

2 7 N-B3, PxP; 8 BPxP, B-N5 is the sequence. White's impressively expanded, though also somewhat shaky, center is under fire. How is White to capitalize his advantage in terrain, before his midsection crumbles? This is the perpetual problem of the obstreperously hypermodern opening.

3 9 P-B5 sets the men in motion. Black is prodded from his complacency and the picture changes. Immediate, tactical plays overrule the strategic concept. There follows 9 . . . N-Q4; 10 Q-N3, BxN; 11 PxB, P-K3. Black wishes to cash in on the weakness in White's King's camp.

4 12 NxN cuts down the wood and takes the sting out of any brewing counter-attack. Because the ending is unfavorable, Black does not swap Queens. He gambles on molesting the White King. There follows 12 . . . Q-R5ch; 13 K-K2, PxN. White's Kingdom for a Rook is the tempting (?) offer.

5 White accepts a Pawn with 14 QxNP and Black plays 14 . . . Qx QP. Then White goes after the Black King. 15 Q-B8ch, K-K2; 16 B-N5ch, P-B3; 17 QxPch, N-Q2 are the moves. Both Kings are insecure, and it is a question of who brings out his attacking forces more rapidly. It is White's turn.

6 18 PxPch opens new lines, and Black plays 18 . . . BxP. Then follows 19 Q-Q6ch. Black is compelled to retreat and cut the communication of his Rooks—a decisive factor here and now. 19 . . . K-K1 is Black's move. Both Kings eye each other reproachfully on the open King file.

7 White brings up reinforcements, as 20 R-Q1 drives the opposing Queen with tempo. Black replies 20 . . . QxPch, and White interposes 21 R-Q2. Again, the Queen must move. Now it is 21 . . . Q-B6. White's last two moves have enabled him to swing the favorable balance of power.

8 White initiates a double threat with 22 QxP. It is too late to parry everything. Black goes in for a mad scramble. 22 . . . BxB is the move. White plays 23 QxRch and Black replies 23 . . . K-K2. Now it is necessary to consolidate, if it is at all possible to consolidate.

9 24 Q-K4ch is the right move in that direction. Black holds on to everything with 24 . . . K-Q1. Comes a positional move: 25 R-B2, reinforcing the dangerous passed Queen Bishop Pawn. Black retreats 25 . . . Q-B3. With an active majority of men, White overwhelms his adversary.

10 26 P-B6 does the trick. Suddenly the passed Pawn has assumed major significance. Vainly, Black pins the opposing Queen with 26 . . . R-K1. Who would dream that the game would be over with one fell blow? White replies 27 P-B7ch. The mite is now mighty. Black resigns.

15

Center Counter Defense

THE Center Counter—*1* P-K4, P-Q4—is an attempt by Black to wrest away White's endowed initiative on the very first move. This is in direct conflict with theory.

Axiomatic—and almost comical—is the proposition in the chess opening that, when White plays *1* P-Q4, he sets his sights for P-K4, and, when he plays *1* P-K4, then P-Q4 is his militant goal. The moves P-K4 and P-Q4 (or *vice versa*) cannot be successfully enforced in consecutive order, when both players immediately fight for control of the center. For the scales of opening play are so delicately balanced that the sequence would cost as little as a tempo or as much as a Pawn. By the same token, Black may not respond to *1* P-Q4 with . . . P-K4 or to *1* P-K4 with . . . P-Q4. Material or time will be his price.

On this ground, the Center Counter, which violates that tenet, is doomed from the beginning. For, on the second move, Black presents White with a valuable tempo. Yet, since there is no known way for the elected defender to seize the lead without some kind of investment, the offer of a tempo is his calculated risk.

The Center Counter was first recommended by Lucena (1497). Since then it has cropped up time and again in serious play, with intermittent success. A favorite with Mieses, it has enabled him to chalk up innumerable and brilliant victories. Because new ways to capitalize the extra tempo have come to light, however, the popularity of the defense is on the wane.

The defense arises as follows:

1 **P-K4   P-Q4**

The Center Counter. Black's Queen Pawn strikes White's King Pawn, suggesting an exchange of Pawns. The idea behind Black's move is the opening of the Queen file, the release of the Queen Bishop for immediate action and the relocation of the Queen to a dominating position, bearing on the center of the board.

The idea is good insofar as its attainment leads to a free and easy game. Its execution, however, is impossible to achieve with proper play on White's part.

2 **PxP**   . . . .

The only way to attempt a refutation of Black's move. 2 P-K5 sets no problems, for Black is able to develop all his forces with facility. 2 N-QB3 is a poor alternative since it grants Black the option of advancing . . . P-Q5 or capturing . . . PxP. He obtains an easy game in either case. 2 P-Q4 is a needless gambit which compels White to pursue the recovery of a Pawn.

2 . . . .　QxP

This is the main variation. Black's Queen momentarily enjoys a dominant role.

Alternatives here are 2 . . . N-KB3 and the gambit, 2 . . . P-QB3. In both instances, White obtains the superior position. For example, if 2 . . . N-KB3; 3 P-QB4, P-B3; 4 P-Q4, PxP; 5 N-QB3, N-B3; 6 B-N5, P-K3; 7 P-B5. With proper procedure, White nurses his Queen-side Pawn majority into a real threat. Or, if 2 . . . P-QB3; 3 PxP, NxP, Black's minimal lead in development is insufficient for the Pawn minus.

3 N-QB3

The Knight develops and attacks the adverse Queen, thereby gaining a move. Thus, instead of the usual initiative which is White's lot, White picks up an extra tempo.

3 . . . . Q-QR4

Black's idea is to exercise pressure on his diagonal, QR4-K8, as well as on the open Queen file later on. The issue is whether the pressure will offset the effect of White's superior development.

The unappetizing alternative is 3 . . . Q-Q1. On the face of it, this move is ruled out, because the time in bringing out and retreating the Queen is spent to no avail. The opening of the Queen file, of itself, is insufficient compensation for White's superior development.

4 P-Q4 . . . .

White may venture on the gambit 4 P-QN4 at this point. In that case, White promotes his development at a rapid pace at the expense of a Pawn. While the gambit may be sound, there is no need to speculate so long as the normal moves produce an excellent position.

The text move controls the important central squares.

4 . . . . N-KB3

A temporizing, developing move, bearing on the center. Black hopes to bring out all his men soon and crack down on White's Queen Pawn.

An interesting alternative is 4 . . . P-K4. With correct play, however, this falls short because the game opens wide, while White is still ahead in development. On the other hand, it is best for White to familiarize himself with its possibilities. The line might run as follows: *4 . . .* P-K4; *5* N-B3 (accent on development), B-QN5; *6* B-Q2, B-N5; *7* B-K2, PxP; *8* NxP, Q-K4; *9* QN-N5! QBxB; *10* QxB, BxB*ch;* *11* KxB, QxQ*ch;* *12* KxQ, N-QR3; *13* KR-K1, O-O-O; *14* NxP*ch,* K-N1; *15* N/7-B6*ch.* This is from a game Tarrasch—Mieses, Gothenburg, 1920. White won the endgame.

After *4 . . .* P-K4; *5* PxP, Black is able to equalize as follows: *. . .* B-QN5, *6* N-B3, B-N5; *7* B-K2, N-QB3; *8* O-O, KN-K2. Black must recover the Pawn.

5 N-B3 . . . .

Normal development, bearing on the center.

6 . . . . B-N5

Neutralizing the Knight's effect on the center and clearing the path for an eventual Queen-side castling, with pressure on White's Queen Pawn.

6 P-KR3! . . . .

Putting the question to the Bishop.

6 . . . . B-R4

The Bishop retreats to maintain the pin on the Knight. If *6 . . .* BxN; *7* QxB, White not only maintains control of the center but also has the advantage of two Bishops.

7 P-KN4! . . . .

This wing demonstration liberates the King Knight at the expense of White's King-side Pawn structure. Since White is ahead in development, however, he wishes to capitalize this plus before Black can consolidate. By doing so, he hopes that the weakness of the Pawn structure will play little part in the future proceedings.

7 . . . . B-N3
8 N-K5 . . . .

The Knight is now in a dominant post and threatens to molest the Black Queen, by retreating to QB4. The Queen is shy a good escape square.

8 . . . . **P-B3**

Creating an exit for the Queen.

9 **N-B4** . . . .

Compelling the Queen to retreat and to relinquish the pin on the Queen Knight.

9 . . . . **Q-B2**

The Queen's haven. 9 . . . Q-Q1 is an admission that the entire Queen Maneuver—Q-Q4-QR4—is pointless.

10 **Q-B3!** . . . .

The star move in White's play. The objectives of the sacrifice are:

(*a*) to support the Queen Bishop at KB4. This, in turn, will promote White's development at Black's expense;

(*b*) to clear the first rank in readiness for Queen-side castling;

(*c*) to bolster and make more potent White's contemplated King-side Pawn advance by nullifying Black's K5. Thus, this square will not be available to the Knight or Bishop in the event one or the other is attacked.

10 . . . .   BxP

On other moves, 11 B-B4, followed by 12 O-O-O, leaves White with an overwhelming position.

The text move is definitely faulty and Black's play may be considered to be refuted.

11 B-B4   . . . .

11 . . . .   Q-Q1

Because Black's last move loses immediately, the less appetizing 11 . . . Q-Q2 is worthy of consideration. Even that, however, leaves Black in dire straits: 11 . . . Q-Q2; 12 R-B1, B-N3; 13 N-K5, Q-Q1; 14 P-Q5. If now 14 . . . PxP; 15 B-N5ch, QN-Q2; 16 NxQP, White wins at least a piece by the threat of 17 NxNch and 18 BxNch. On 16 . . . Q-R4ch, there follows 17 P-N4! In this line, if 13 . . . QxQP; 14 N-N5 is a crushing rejoinder: . . . Q-K5ch; 15 QxQ, BxQ; 16 N-B7ch, K-Q1; 17 NxR, BxR; 18 NxPch and 19 NxR—also 16 P-B3, N-R3; 17 PxB, PxN; 18 BxPch, N-Q2 (forced) 19 BxNch.

12 Q-K2!!   . . . .

Even though the movement of the Queen twice in the opening is contrary to principle, it is, in this case, the sockdolager. And the apparent violation is based on Black's complete misconception of the strategy of the opening.

12 . . . . **B-N3**

If *12 . . .* QxP; *13* B-K5 wins the unguarded Bishop.

13 **N-Q6ch.** . . . .

The point of White's 12th. Black's King Pawn is pinned and his King is prodded into insecurity.

13 . . . . **K-Q2**
14 **NxNP** . . . .

Black is lost. White has recovered the Pawn.

The entire line is based on the game Horowitz–Kibberman, Warsaw, 1935, which ended as follows:

14 . . . Q-N3; *15* N-B5*ch*, K-B1; *16* B-N2, P-K3; *17* O-O, N-Q4; *18* NxN, BPxN; *19* QR-B1, K-Q1; *20* B-N5*ch!* B-K2; *21* BxB*ch*, KxB; *22* BxP, N-Q2; *23* BxR, RxB; *24* NxN, KxN; *25* KR-Q1, Q-N2; *26* P-Q5, PxP; *27* Q-K5, Resigns.

Conclusions

While the strategic concept of the Center Counter Defense is laudable, its tactical execution is impossible of fulfillment. In the line where Black plays *4 . . .* P-K4 (see note to Black's fourth move), Black succeeds in obtaining a free game and a comparatively easy development for all his men. His position bogs down, however, because he is two tempi behind in development. If some way can be found to bolster this plan, the defense may yet be tenable.

Chess Movie

COUNTER COUNTERED

A course in winning chess tactics is the fare of this classic brevity. Knight forks, pins, double attacks are rampant. To boot, the strategic concept of simultaneous attack and defense is exemplified. Duras, White, finally belays his pugnacious opponent, Spielmann, by a well-directed grenade. Vienna, 1907, is the scene of play. Follow the game "movie style." *1* P-K4, P-Q4; *2* PxP, QxP; *3* N-QB3, Q-QR4; *4* P-Q4, N-KB3. (*See diagram No. 1.*)

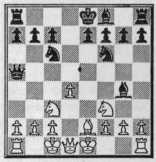

1 There follows 5 N-B3, B-N5. White omits any King-side Pawn demonstration. The slow, positional 6 B-K2 is his move. This gives Black the opportunity to show his stuff. With *6 . . . N-B3*, Black readies for Queen-side castling and powerful pressure against the Queen Pawn.

2 Anticipating the attack on the Pawn, Duras plays the prophylactic 7 B-K3 and Spielmann counters with 7 . . . O-O-O. A Knight maneuver further wards off the pressure: 8 N-Q2. There follows 8 . . . BxB; 9 QxB, Q-KB4. Observe that a Knight fork had immunized the weakling Queen Pawn.

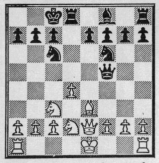

3 Duras swings his Knight to the long side of the board with *10 N-N3*, and Spielmann furthers his development with *10 . . . P-K3*. Now follows: *11 P-QR3, . . . B-Q3*. In order to contain the battle on one side, White castles long: *12 O-O-O*. Black responds *12 . . . N-Q4. 13 . . . NxN* is his threat.

4 *13 N-R4* is the follow-up. White's men begin to close in on the Black monarch. Black counters with *13 . . . P-K4* and there follows the exchange *14 PxP, BxKP*. White pre-empts a strategic square with *15 N/4-B5* and Black consolidates his position with *15 . . . N-N3*.

5 Duras attempts to force a weakening on the flank with *16 P-QR4*, and Spielmann parries with *16 . . . P-QR4*. Now Duras drives the Black Queen with *17 P-N4*, and the Queen retreats: *17 . . . Q-B3*. There follows *18 P-QB3, KR-K1*. As yet, no perceptible incursion is under way. But wait.

6 *19 NxNP* upsets Black's equanimity. A free-for-all ensues: *19 . . . Rx Rch; 20 RxR, BxBP*, and both Kings are in jeopardy. The complications are thick and the action fast. Who will come out on top of this perplexing maze? Whose attack will hit home hardest?—that is the vital question.

7 Duras retreats *21 N/7-B5* and opens a direct avenue to the Black monarch. Spielmann counters with *21 . . . N-N5.* There follows *22 P-N5, Q-K4.* Both sides are on tenterhooks. To attack and defend simultaneously is a difficult feat. One slip, and the game falls by the wayside.

8 Now comes the prelude to one of the finest combinations of the sixty-four squares. White plays *23 NxP,* heading for the general direction of the opposing King. Offhand, it has the earmarks of a trap. (Black dare not play *23 . . . QxN* on account of *24 Q-N4ch.*) Black plays *23 . . . P-R4.*

9 Now, however, White can capture the loose Bishop and he does with *24 PxB.* Black continues with *24 . . . QxPch* and perforce White plays *25 K-N1.* There evidently is no reason why Black cannot take the Knight at this moment. So Black plays *25 . . . QxN,* satisfied that the game is in the bag.

10 Maybe it is and maybe it isn't. One thing is certain, White's King is just as exposed to flailing blows as Black's. Who would dream that in one fell move the game is over? *26 R-Q8ch* is the move!! and Black topples from the *Sessel.* He cannot capture the Rook safely. Black resigns.